SELF PUBLISHING SECRET SAUCE

Write High-Profit Books Readers Want Using Data to Verify Your Ideas

MICHELLE KULP

TABLE OF CONTENTS

INTRODUCTION 1

CHAPTER 1: REVERSE ENGINEERING YOUR BOOK
FOR SUCCESS... 7

CHAPTER 2: THE BIG GLITCH IN AMAZON'S
SYSTEM... 21

CHAPTER 3: CREATING A KILLER TITLE 31

CHAPTER 4: LAUNCH OR PERISH.. 43

CHAPTER 5: THE SECRET TO STAYING A
BESTSELLER 55

CHAPTER 6: THE BESTSELLER CHECKLIST 79

CHAPTER 7: WHY YOU SHOULD WRITE MORE
THAN ONE BOOK... 85

CHAPTER 8: HOW TO WRITE SHORT BOOKS FAST 91

CHAPTER 9: HOW TO GET A BOOK ON WALL STREET
JOURNAL AND USA TODAY BESTSELLER LISTS 103

CHAPTER 10: CLOSING THOUGHTS.................................. 111

BONUS: MICHELLE'S PRIVATE AND VETTED
ROLODEX.. 115

INTRODUCTION

Every successful business has a *Secret Sauce.*

McDonald's, Coke, Nike, Netflix, Amazon, Zoom, DoorDash, Grubhub, and thousands more, both new and old, have a secret sauce that is the cornerstone to their success.

If you want to become a successful author and achieve long-term success, you too should have a secret sauce.

Callisto Media, a company that has been around for close to 10 years, has consistently published "bestsellers" that have long-term success. Using big-data analysis, Callisto determines where there's an audience clamoring for a non-fiction book that doesn't exist yet, then hires someone to write it.

A couple of years ago, one of my clients was approached by Callisto Media to write a book. They provided the topic, title, and subtitle and paid her under $10K to write it. She was given a 60-day timeline after which she submitted the manuscript to Callisto and collected the money. Although her name is on the book, she is no longer invested or connected to the book's success and receives no royalties from the book's sales.

Callisto Media is finding what the market wants and where there is a huge hole they can fill. Then, they fill that hole with a new book that will ultimately become a bestseller because they know how to market the book. Callisto seeks out established, credible, and high-level experts to write books and they get paid for their services (unlike ghostwriters who receive no recognition for writing a book).

The point is they have a "Secret Sauce" and have created a successful empire using this proprietary method. The good news is we can learn from Callisto Media when it comes to writing our books.

Chris Fox, author of *"Write to Market"* says:

Many authors write, then market. Successful authors write TO market. They start by figuring out how to give readers what they want, and that process begins before writing word one of your book.

Before implementing his "write to market" philosophy, Chris Fox was a broke author. Now, he has a 7-figure author income with both fiction books and non-fiction books.

In this book, my goal is to teach you how to reverse engineer your book, figure out what the market wants *before* you write your book, and verify your idea with data. Once you have a "high-profit" book topic, then I'll give you the *Secret Sauce* to getting every book you write on the bestsellers list so readers can find your book and you can get more sales.

My very first client in my Bestselling Author program was a former technical writer for the *Washington Post.* In 2013, we launched her book to the bestsellers list; now, seven years later, her book is still on the top of the bestsellers list, and she has created what she calls "mortgage money" as royalties from her books pays all of her house expenses.

MY EXPERIMENT WRITING A BOOK A MONTH

Last year, I read an article on **Written Word Media** that said the average $100K author has 28 books in their catalog. At the time, I only had eight books published, and they were pretty old and outdated. I was intrigued by this article and decided to test this theory by writing a book a month. In January 2020, I started writing a book a month and have been doing so ever since. My goal is to have 28 books published and to create a six-figure passive income. I'm happy to tell you that I am currently generating $2,300 a month in passive income and am on my way to achieving my goal of making six figures from my books.

I share my entire process and system in my #1 bestselling book, *28 Books to $100K*, so I won't go over all the details here. If you want my free templates for the book a month system, you can join my private Facebook group and download them from there.

Before I write my book each month, I have learned from experience to always do my research first. I reverse engineer the idea I have and make sure the data supports the book I want to write, and then I add the *Secret Sauce* so I can make every book I write a bestseller.

Some of you may be wondering, "Why is it important to become a bestseller?

I think that's a fair question, so let me give you an analogy…

Let's say you want to buy a business book; you're not sure exactly *which* business book, but you know you want *a* business book. So, you hop in your car and head to the bookstore. As you enter the store, you see a beautiful display with a sign that says, "NEW BUSINESS BOOKS." You are instantly attracted to the display and this section of new business books, so you walk over and start browsing. You find a book you love, purchase it, and go home excited to read your new book!

That's similar to how bestseller lists work online – particularly on Amazon, where there are hundreds of thousands of business books. The question is: How do readers find these business books (or other genres) they are looking for if they only have a general topic in mind?

The answer is: They search the bestsellers lists until they find a book that speaks to them or solves a problem they are having.

To have success with your book, you must have visibility. You can write the best book in the world, but if readers can't find it, your bank account will remain empty.

Not being on a bestsellers list is like having your book on the bottom shelf, in the furthest corner of the bookstore, where no one can see or find it.

On the other hand, having your book on a bestsellers list gives you the same benefits as having your book on the front display of the bookstore with lots of eyeballs and visibility.

When you understand how to use data in your favor to write books, and you know how to launch your books to the bestsellers list using the *Secret Sauce* I will be sharing, you are positioning yourself for long-term success.

Of course, there is no guarantee a book will be successful. However, having the *Self Publishing Secret Sauce* will put you light years ahead of other self-published authors vying for readers' attention.

Here's some of what you will learn in *Self Publishing Secret Sauce*:

- Why BISAC codes are keeping your book invisible
- The BIG glitch in Amazon's system a librarian would understand
- Why having the wrong categories will block you from bestseller status
- The big secrets Amazon will never tell you about that prevent your book from being on any bestsellers list
- Why keywords matter and why 95% of authors get them wrong
- How to dominate Bestseller lists
- How to become a Wall Street Journal and USA Today Bestselling Author
- Why you should never write only one book
- Rapid Writing Secrets
- And more!

So, if you're ready to learn the *Self Publishing Secret Sauce* from someone who has written over 20 books, currently has more than a dozen books on the Amazon bestsellers lists, is on her way to making six figures in royalties from writing a "book a month," and has launched over 250 #1 bestselling books for clients in my Bestselling Author program, then let's get started…

CHAPTER 1

REVERSE ENGINEERING
YOUR BOOK FOR SUCCESS

Your mission, should you choose to accept it, is to come up with a *high-profit topic*. A high-profit topic is one that the data shows people are searching for and has high monthly earnings for that keyword.

A low-profit topic, on the other hand, is one that the data shows is not frequently searched for on Amazon and does not have high monthly earnings.

Over the years, I've had the privilege of working with over 250 clients, many of whom came to me with what seemed like "great" book ideas.

Unfortunately, through years of experience, I've learned that it doesn't matter what you like or what you think will make a great book – **all that matters is the data.**

Let me share an example of a client who came to me with what seemed like a great idea for a book…except, it wasn't.

I received a strategy session application from a couple who wanted to write a book about English Cottage Gardens. We had a lovely conversation, and I told them I would research the topic and get back to them.

It seemed like a good topic, but I had never done a book for a client in this genre, so I needed to do my research first.

I believe in numbers and data more than guessing.

I use Publisher Rocket for all of my research; it's a paid software that will save you a lot of time because it gives you important data that will help you write a high-profit book rather than a low-profit book.

My research on Publisher Rocket revealed few searches for this topic:

Keywords	Number of Searches per month on Amazon
English cottage gardens	Less than 100
English cottage gardens books	Less than 100
English cottage garden	Less than 100
Cottage garden ideas	Less than 100
Cottage garden flowers	Less than 100

Additionally, *English Cottage Gardens* books on Amazon were not making much money either (I used KDSpy to find the sales numbers for these books).

Now, these were very nice people, and I could have signed them into my high-ticket program and let them write a book on

English Cottage Gardens (an area in which they were experts), however, I don't take on clients unless I feel strongly that they have a high-profit topic that can be positioned for long-term success.

I suggested to these potential clients that they write a book on **RAISED BED and CONTAINER GARDENING** after discovering during my research this was a very hot and, most importantly, high-profit topic.

My research on Publisher Rocket revealed there were hundreds of searches for this topic:

Keywords	Number of Searches per month on Amazon
Raised bed gardening books	1,161
Raised bed gardening containers	493
Container gardening book	548
Gardening in containers	626
Gardening for beginners	540
Vegetable gardening for beginners	848
Gardening for beginners herbs	849

The results for this topic were much better than "English Cottage Gardens." Moreover, I found books on this topic making $25,000 per month (one of the top books on the best-sellers list ironically was published by Callisto Media who I mentioned earlier). I was pleasantly surprised!

These potential clients hired me, and I agreed to help them write a book on raised bed and container gardening. I'm happy to tell you that during our 2-day launch, 5800+ people downloaded their book. One day after the launch, my clients' book was on multiple #1 paid bestsellers lists as well as many others.

Their book is now positioned for success and their sales are growing each month as we add more *Secret Sauce*.

Using research and data just like Callisto Media does, we reverse-engineered a bestselling book!

So, what would you like to write a book about?

10 Steps to Selecting Your Book Topic

1. **Select A Topic in Which You Are an Expert In** – Here are some ideas: What obstacles have you overcome? What skills do you possess that others would be interested in? What successful businesses or careers have you had? Write what you know, but always do the research to make sure the market is looking for this information. If you are writing a nonfiction book, you want to figure out the million-dollar problem people are having and position your book as the solution.

2. **Invest in Publisher Rocket** – Research keywords that you think people are using when searching for books on your topic. Record this information in a document or spreadsheet and save it. After you write your book, you will use your top seven keywords when publishing it. (I'll explain how to do this shortly.)

3. **Check out the Competition** – After you find your keywords in Publisher Rocket, click on the green button to the right of the keyword results labeled "Competition" to view the top-selling books on that topic.

Note: There are two ways you can find out how many copies a book has sold. I use KDSpy which shows me the number of sales in the past 30 days for eBooks and print books. Alternatively, you can look at the book's *sales ranking*, which can be found on the 'Product Details' section of the book page on Amazon. Write down the sales ranking number and then go to the free Sales Rank Calculator provided by the founder of Publisher Rocket, Dave Chesson: https://kindlepreneur.com/amazon-kdp-sales-rank-calculator/ to see the number of books that were sold to achieve that ranking.

4. **Do Your Keyword Research** – [Step-by-Step Instructions are below]. *Publisher Rocket* will show you how many people are searching for specific keywords on Amazon, which is valuable information. Keywords with a minimum of a few hundred searches per month could be a good topic to write about. I like to find seven keyword phrases that have 300-2000+ searches per month on Amazon. Additionally, when you look at books in your genre on Amazon, make sure they are making at least $1,000+ per month; the higher the profits, the better. This way you can assure you have a high-profit topic.

5. **Check Out Your Competition's Bad Reviews -** Read the bad reviews of the top-selling books in your genre and make notes on ways you can improve on those complaints with your book. I've even come up with ideas for my own books from reading bad reviews!

6. **Browse the Table of Contents from Other Bestselling Books** – If your book has good profit potential at this point, review the table of contents of other books to get some ideas for writing and positioning your book.

   Did you know that you cannot copyright a book title? You could write a book right now and use the title *7 Habits of Highly Successful People*. In fact, many authors use successful titles as a springboard for their own titles. For example, *Write and Grow Rich* is a take-off of Napoleon Hill's *Think and Grow Rich*.

7. **Look on Reddit** – Search for posts on your topic that have a lot of engagement and high-volume groups. You could also look on platforms like Facebook, LinkedIn, Instagram, etc. Book ideas are everywhere!

8. **See If There Are Any TED Talks on YouTube About Your Topic**. Try to find ones that have a high number of views and maybe use a similar title.

9. **Poll Your Target Audience**. If you have an email list, Facebook group, or other social media group, you can do a poll and ask your target audience. Note: Asking outside of your target audience won't give you accurate results.

10. **Create Several Titles and Run a Survey to Pick the Best One.** Once you come up with several potential titles for your book, use www.surveymonkey.com/ (which is free) to

see what your audience prefers. If you want a paid option for polls on cover designs or titles, go to:

https://www.pickfu.com/blog/testing-book-titles-covers/ (I go over titling your book in more detail later).

For ideas on coming up with a title for your book, read the article at: https://kindlepreneur.com/how-to-title-a-book-with-good-book-titles/

I want you to write down three of your top ideas based on your expertise that get your juices flowing.

Top 3 Book Ideas

1. _____

2. _____

3. _____

Now it's time to gather the data for the topic of your book. Even if you have an idea for your book's title, you need to research the keywords people search for on Amazon when looking for this type of book.

If possible, use the keywords people are searching for in your title or subtitle, and include them in your book description.

USING KEYWORDS IN BOOK TITLES

One of my clients, Lisa Phillips came to me in 2018 and wanted to write a book about investing in rental properties for beginners. We came up with a lot of clever and fun titles, but once I showed her the keyword research, she said something brilliant:

"Let's just use the top searched keyword phrase as the title."

The top search on Amazon for her niche based on the data we collected was:

Investing in Rental Properties for Beginners

We didn't need to come up with something new or clever; we used the exact keyword phrase that people were searching for on Amazon.

Lisa is one of my top clients, and this one book has created a multiple six-figure business for her. She makes anywhere from $3,000 to $5,000 per month on book sales alone, and she has several backend courses and coaching programs she sells:

https://lisa-phillips.thinkific.com/

I've abandoned many book ideas after researching ideas for books I wanted to write. The data I found just didn't support me investing my energy, time, and money in writing that book on what essentially was a low profit topic.

Minimize Your Risk and Increase Your Chances for Long-Term Success

Of course, you cannot predict how well any book will do, but taking the time to do this research puts your book in a great position to do well.

Let's go over the seven steps you need in order to reverse engineer your book and make sure you have a high profit topic.

1. Write down your top three ideas.

2. For each idea, write down 10 keywords/phrases you think people are searching for to find this type of book.

3. Invest in Publisher Rocket and look at the data to see how many people are searching for this keyword.

4. As you do this research, make note of new keywords that are revealed that you didn't previously consider.

5. Write down at least seven keywords that have a search volume over 300+ per month on Amazon.

6. If you can't find seven keywords or the search volume is under 100 for many of your keywords, then you probably have a low-profit topic.

7. If you have a low-profit topic, move on to your next idea and repeat the research.

Next, I'm going to take you through the steps I used when researching keywords for my book, *28 Books to $100K.*

First, I wrote down the keywords I thought people might be searching for.

- Book launch
- How to make money with a book

- Passive income

- 6 figures

- How to market a book

Next, I entered keywords on Publisher Rocket and found these winners and losers:

Book Launch – under 100 (LOW PROFIT)

6-Figure Author – 1082 searches with average monthly earnings of $2,297 (WINNER!)

How to Make a Living with Your Writing – 315 Searches with average monthly earnings of $10,173 (WINNER!)

How to Make a Living Writing – 1,111 Searches, but the average monthly earnings is only $269, so it is LOW PROFIT

6 Figures a Year Writing– 8,140 Searches on Amazon with average monthly earnings of $24,034 (WINNER!)

How to Market My Book – 839 Searches on Amazon with average monthly earnings of $18,779 (WINNER!)

How to Market as an Author – 136 Searches (which is low), with high average monthly earnings of $8201 (Could go either way, but I decided it was a Winner and to use it)

Self-Publishing for Beginners – 615 Searches with high average monthly earnings of $8892 (WINNER!)

Making Passive Income Writing Books – 163 Searches per month on Amazon (a little low), with high average monthly earnings of $5660 (Could go either way, but I decided it was a Winner and to use it)

Passive Income – 1255 (TOO BROAD; NOT TARGETED FOR AUTHORS)

How to Make Money Writing Nonfiction – Under 100 searches (LOW PROFIT)

It can take a couple of hours to do this research, but it's well worth it. Sometimes, it's a good idea to double-check keywords by going to Amazon and typing the keyword in the search bar to see what comes up. Some keywords may not mean what you think and could have a double meaning.

Keep in mind that the data you gather is fluid, and these numbers are in real-time. If I check these keywords six months from now, I'm sure the data will change.

So, it's a good idea to update your keywords every few months.

Maximize Keywords When Publishing

You are allowed seven keywords when you publish, so doing this research serves two purposes:

1. Determine if the data supports writing a book on this topic

2. Selecting exact keywords to use when self-publishing on Amazon

The biggest mistake I see clients make when selecting keywords is choosing ones that are too broad. Listed below are examples of "not so good" keywords:

- Nonfiction books
- Fiction books
- Business
- Self-help

These keywords have thousands of searches on Amazon, but they are too broad and too general. If you want to attract your ideal reader, you need to niche down.

Now that you understand how to reverse engineer your book for a high-profit topic by researching the keywords first, I want you to have some context and understand the big glitch in Amazon's system when publishing – and this has to do with categories…

CHAPTER 2

THE BIG GLITCH IN AMAZON'S SYSTEM

In 2011, I published my first book on Amazon and naïvely thought people would magically find my book. I believed all I had to do was write a quality book, hit publish, and the rest would happen on its own.

Guess what? A year after I hit *publish*, I had ZERO sales!

So, I did some research to understand how readers find books and how authors get on multiple bestsellers lists. I discovered that Amazon had a big glitch in their system.

When you publish a paperback book, you have to use Book Industry Standards and Communications (BISAC) codes, which are universal codes for categories used by publishers and book distributors. Visit this page to find BISAC codes for any topic: https://bisg.org/page/BISACEdition

Below is a screenshot of some BISAC codes for Business:

BUS000000	**BUSINESS & ECONOMICS** / General
BUS001000	**BUSINESS & ECONOMICS** / Accounting / General
BUS001010	**BUSINESS & ECONOMICS** / Accounting / Financial
BUS001020	**BUSINESS & ECONOMICS** / Accounting / Governmental
	BUSINESS & ECONOMICS / Accounting / International *see* International / Accounting
BUS001040	**BUSINESS & ECONOMICS** / Accounting / Managerial
BUS001050	**BUSINESS & ECONOMICS** / Accounting / Standards (GAAP, IFRS, etc.)
BUS002000	**BUSINESS & ECONOMICS** / Advertising & Promotion
BUS003000	**BUSINESS & ECONOMICS** / Auditing
BUS004000	**BUSINESS & ECONOMICS** / Banks & Banking
BUS114000	**BUSINESS & ECONOMICS** / Bitcoin & Cryptocurrencies *
BUS005000	**BUSINESS & ECONOMICS** / Bookkeeping
BUS006000	**BUSINESS & ECONOMICS** / Budgeting
BUS007000	**BUSINESS & ECONOMICS** / Business Communication / General
BUS007010	**BUSINESS & ECONOMICS** / Business Communication / Meetings & Presentations
BUS008000	**BUSINESS & ECONOMICS** / Business Ethics

The general BISAC codes are broad categories, although some narrow down into subcategories. For example:

- BUS007010: Business & Economics/Business Communication/Meetings & Presentations

Publishers have used BISAC codes for decades to categorize print books, but that's NOT the system Amazon uses.

Amazon has their own system for categorizing books with topics and categories similar to BISAC codes, but also have thousands more subcategories that are NOT available to select when you publish your book.

THE BIG GLITCH

The BIG glitch in Amazon's system is when you publish your book, you can only choose two categories, which are similar to BISAC Codes and very competitive. Usually, these are too broad and general, and using them may prevent your book from getting on any bestsellers list.

My first book had zero sales after one year because I chose two broad categories and I was unable to rank on a bestsellers list or get any visibility with those "wrong" categories.

Why?

If you select the "nonfiction" category when you publish your book, then you are competing with the top 100 nonfiction authors of all time who are selling thousands and maybe millions of books. So, the chance of your book getting on the "nonfiction" bestsellers list is slim to none.

We already established why you want to be on the bestsellers lists, right?

Because you need visibility; you need eyeballs, and you want your book to be on the most searched lists on Amazon (which is akin to being in the display at the front of a brick-and-mortar bookstore).

Even if you choose a category from your KDP publishing account that has a subcategory, such as Business/Entrepreneurship, it is still going to be too competitive for you to rank in that category as a new, self-published author.

SIX SECRETS ABOUT AMAZON CATEGORIES

Secret #1 – Your book can be included in up to 10 categories on Amazon, although you only have the option to select two when you publish.

Secret #2: The categories you select when you publish are NOT the same categories and subcategories you see when searching bestseller lists on Amazon. There are thousands more categories outside of your publishing account and on the Amazon platform.

Secret #3: You must determine which categories you can rank for to get on the top of the bestseller lists and submit a customer support ticket asking Amazon to add your book to the additional categories.

Secret #4: Before selecting additional categories, decide if you are going to launch your book to the free bestsellers list or the paid bestsellers list because the sales ranking numbers will be different. So, your category choices will be different.

Secret #5: You must give Amazon the complete category "thread" you want to be added to. For example: Kindle ebooks> business & money>job hunting & careers>vocational guidance (I had Amazon add this category for my book *How to Find Your Passion*).

Secret #6: You must look at sales ranking numbers to determine which categories to put your book in so you can rank #1 in that category during your launch.

After I decided I was doing a paid launch at $.99, for my book, *How to find Your Passion*, I researched the categories and sent the following customer support ticket to Amazon from my KDP account:

Hello,

Can you add the following categories for my book, *How to Find Your Passion*, ASIN B083XL67GZ:

Kindle ebooks > business & money > job hunting & careers >vocational guidance

Kindle ebooks>health, fitness & dieting>personal health>work-related health

Kindle ebooks>education & teaching>test preparation>careers

Kindle ebooks>business & money>entrepreneurship & small business>franchise

Kindle ebooks>education & teaching>higher & continuing education>graduate school>business

Kindle ebooks>business & money>job hunting & careers>interviewing

Thank you,

Michelle Kulp

I didn't *guess* which categories to put my book in; I used the paid software, Bestseller Ranking Pro, to find categories where I could rank at the top of the bestsellers list on launch day.

Right now, there are over 10,000 categories on Amazon which is why I use Bestseller Ranking Pro to save time!

You can watch this video by Tom Corson Knowles, the creator of Bestseller Ranking Pro, that explains why category selection is critically important for your book and placement on a bestsellers list: https://bestsellerrankingpro.com.

**If you use my affiliate link to purchase the software, you will save hundreds of dollars on the price of this: https://mkulp--tckpublishing.thrivecart.com/bestseller-ranking-pro-special-lifetime/

I use Bestseller Ranking Pro to find categories for my clients' books and my own books, so our books can get to the top of the bestseller lists. I used to do this work manually, and it would take me several hours.

I highly recommend Tom's software, but I will share an example of how you can do this manually if you don't want to purchase the software.

Manually Researching Categories

1. Decide whether you want to do a paid or free launch, then search books on either the free bestsellers list or the paid bestsellers list.

2. Find a book similar to yours that is on a bestsellers list. For example, let's say you are doing a "free" launch for a business book about retirement. Go to Amazon and search for retirement books and find a bestselling book. Here is one that I found that is currently a #1 bestseller:

    https://www.amazon.com/Passive-Income-Aggressive-Retirement-Independence-ebook/dp/B081DH1V97/

3. Scroll down the page and look for the "product details" and you'll see the bestsellers sales rank (the lower, the better) and the top three bestseller lists that book is on. Click on one of those bestseller links. Here is the bestsellers list that I am using for this example:

    https://www.amazon.com/gp/bestsellers/digital-text/154933011/ref=pd_zg_hrsr_digital-text

4. When you click on a bestseller link from a book's product page, you will be taken to the paid bestsellers list by default. If you are doing a free launch, make sure you switch over to the free bestseller list for that category:

    https://www.amazon.com/Best-Sellers-Kindle-Store-Real-Estate-Investments/zgbs/digital-text/154933011/ref=zg_bs?_encoding=UTF8&tf=1

5. To determine if you can rank for the #1 bestsellers list, click on the book that is currently #1 on that bestsellers list. For this example, we are looking at the free bestsellers list, and the #1 book on the free list right now has a sales ranking of

5,974. Since I've done over 250 book launches, I know what numbers I can beat and what sales ranking I will get during my book launch. I typically get to the top 100 for sales ranking on a free launch and for a paid launch I can get to 1000 sales ranking. Since this #1 book has a high sales ranking, I know that during my launch I can beat this number. So, I will add my book to this category. It's a winner!

6. I'll go over the launch details and how to do a professional launch in a separate chapter. A launch is a specific time period when you focus all of your marketing efforts to get sales for your book. I usually do a 2-day free book launch for clients or a 1-day paid launch for my own books. The key is to get the highest number of sales (or downloads) for your book in the shortest amount of time.

7. Once my book is published with the two categories I chose while publishing, I research to find six or seven additional categories. Remember, you are allowed a total of 10 categories between your kindle and paperback. Submit the additional category request via a customer support ticket within your KDP account.

8. If you want to learn how to do this, see my course "**28 Books to $100K**" where I have a full online course teaching you how to do this.

Do you see how time consuming it can be to find the right categories for your book? You need to find at least six additional categories after you publish if you want to get on the bestsellers list during your launch.

Categories and keywords are a big part of the *Secret Sauce* to becoming a bestselling author. Of course, you need a great hook for your book, a killer title and subtitle, a magnetic book description, a beautiful cover and of course, as well as professional editing and formatting.

What's important to understand is even if you have all of these things in order, but you don't understand keywords and categories, then your book(s) will probably be INVISIBLE!

That's how important keywords and categories are to your success!

CHAPTER 3

CREATING A KILLER TITLE

You've probably heard the saying, *"Don't judge a book by its cover"*?

However, the fact is, people DO judge a book by its cover, and they will judge a book by its title and subtitle as well. The reality is a boring title can kill book sales. In contrast, a compelling title increases sales and is one of the key components of a bestseller.

Having the right title for a book is the difference between flourishing sales or failing sales, between a book taking off and a book disappearing into the abyss.

A prime example of the importance of a book title comes from E. Haldeman Julius, who owned a publishing company in the 1900s. If a book didn't sell at least 10,000 copies a year, he would send it to the "hospital." There, he would tweak the title until it performed well.

After selling only 6,000 copies of *Gautier's Fleece of Gold*, Haldeman sent it to the "book title hospital" and performed surgery. He relaunched the book with the new title, *The Quest for a Blonde Mistress,* and miraculously, the book sold 50,000 copies that year!

Haldeman believed two things:

1. If the title doesn't tell you what the book is about, it won't do well.

2. You need to tweak the title if your book is not performing.

Every author must learn the art and science of titling a book.

You can be the best writer in the world, but if you have a bad "picker" for selecting your book's title, you will be a broke author with no readers.

So, you're probably wondering, "What's the secret to creating a killer title?"

The key to creating a killer title or bestselling title is whether it can pass this 5-question test:

Question 1: Is the title easy to remember a week later? Is it sticky, memorable, and easy to say out loud?

Question 2: Does the title create curiosity? Does it make you want to know more about the book?

Question 3: Does the title or the subtitle imply value for the reader? Is there an implied promise or an answer to the reader's ultimate question, "What's in it for me?" What are the benefits to the reader?

Question 4: Would a reader feel cool or embarrassed to be seen reading a book with that title? Readers have egos, and titles that people deem offensive or out-of-date and can therefore hinder sales.

Question 5: Does the title help build the author's brand and enable the creation of complementary spin-off resources, such as online programs, consulting, coaching, seminars, and other types of curriculum for non-fiction authors?

These five questions can help you select the perfect title for your book.

So, let's take a look at some bestselling titles! Here are a few Case Studies...

Case Study #1: *Habit Stacking* by S.J. Scott

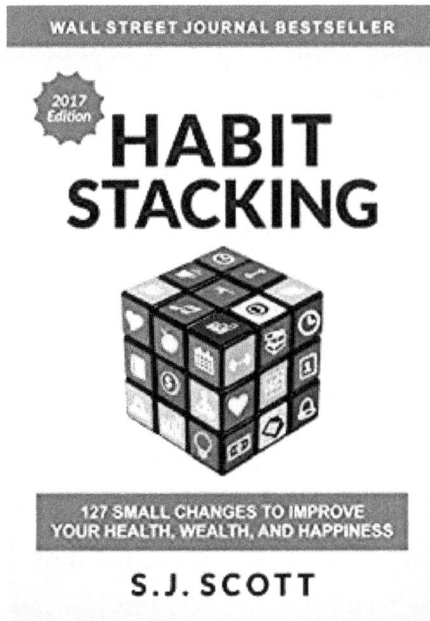

Steve Scott (who also writes under the name "S.J. Scott") has 42+ books published on Amazon. *Habit Stacking* at one time was selling 100 copies a day (3000 copies per month) and making $6000 - $10,000 per month in royalties (just from this one title).

Let's see if Steve's book meets the 5-question test:

Question 1: Is the title easy to remember a week later? Is it sticky, memorable, and easy to say out loud? *Absolutely! Habit Stacking is memorable and easy to say!*

Question 2: Does the title create curiosity? Does it make you want to know more about the book? *Yes, what the heck is habit stacking and what are these 97 life changing habits?*

Question 3: Does the title/subtitle imply value for the reader? Is there an implied promise or an answer to the reader's ultimate question, "What's in it for me?" What are the benefits to the reader? *Stacking 5-minute habits this way can change your life! Yes, it has a strong benefit.*

Question 4: Would a reader feel cool to be seen reading a book with that title? Readers have egos, and titles that people deem offensive or out-of-date and can therefore hinder sales. *Sure! It's a positive book on developing good and smart habits!*

Question 5: Does the title help build the author's brand and enable the creation of complementary spin-off resources, such as online programs, consulting, coaching, seminars, and other types of curriculum for non-fiction authors? *Steve writes his books in a "series," and has other related programs/books that he makes money from.*

Steve also had a professional cover made for his book.

I recommend listening to the Steve Scott Interview if you want to learn how he's making $20,000 to $40,000 per month from his books on Amazon! Here's the link:

http://www.jamesaltucher.com/2014/07/ep-23-go-0-40000-month-writing-home/

Case Study #2: *The Slight Edge* by Jeff Olson

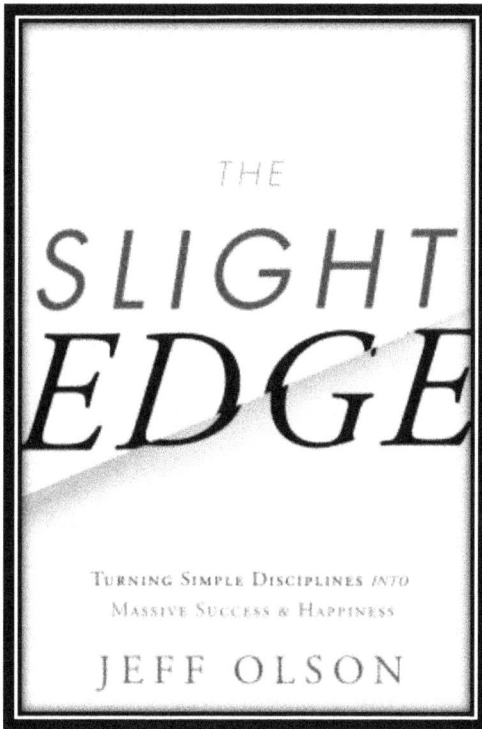

I met Jeff Olson years ago at a network marketing event and he is a great motivational speaker and has managed to keep this book (published originally in 2005) on the paid best sellers list! Right now, this book is selling about 1000 copies per month on Amazon and making over $10,000 per month in royalties!

So, let's see if Jeff's book meets the 5-question test:

Question 1: Is the title easy to remember a week later? Is it sticky, memorable, and easy to say out loud? *Absolutely! The Slight Edge is memorable and easy to say!*

Question 2: Does the title create curiosity? Does it make you want to know more about the book? *Yes, what is the Slight Edge, and how do I get it?*

Question 3: Does the title/subtitle imply value for the reader? Is there an implied promise or an answer to the reader's ultimate question, "What's in it for me?" What are the benefits to the reader? *The benefits are listed in his subtitle: "Turning Simple Disciplines into Massive Success and Happiness."*

Question 4: Would a reader feel cool to be seen reading a book with that title? Readers have egos, and titles that people deem offensive or out-of-date and can therefore hinder sales. *Sure! It's a positive book on success and happiness.*

Question 5: Does the title help build the author's brand and enable the creation of complementary spin-off resources, such as online programs, consulting, coaching, seminars, and other types of curriculum for non-fiction authors? *Jeff Olson has a platform in the network marketing space. Whatever company he is affiliated with, he promotes this book. It applies to all people of all business types...so yes...it leads to Jeff and his business and his products.*

I purchased this book many years ago, and it's awesome! I love it, and it meets the 5-question test.

By the way, his book has 3,370 reviews, which keeps him on the bestsellers list. The more reviews you have, the more Amazon will promote you!

So, thumbs up on this one!

Case Study #3: *The Checklist Manifesto* by Atul Gawande

This book is currently #1 on the Amazon Bestsellers list and is making about $15,000 per month in royalties, selling over 1000 copies per month!

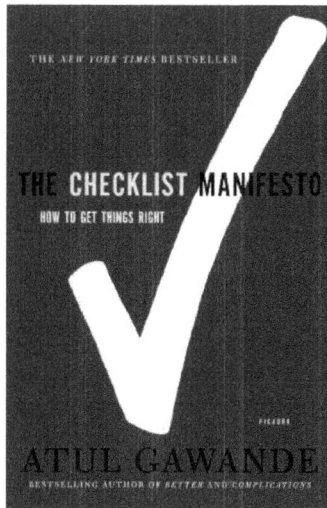

A little about this book: Dr. Gawande is a successful general surgeon with a lot of credibility. He presents example checklists from complex roles like pilots and sky-scraper construction. He walks you through specific use cases, giving interesting examples of how the checklists helped in specific cases. What really hit home was his use of numbers to show the effectiveness of a checklist implemented at several hospitals. One checklist reduced errors by almost forty-five percent (45%). That is huge for any industry.

So, let's see if Dr. Gawande's book meets the 5-question criteria:

Question 1: Is the title easy to remember a week later? Is it sticky, memorable, and easy to say out loud? *Absolutely! The CheckList Manifesto is memorable and easy to say!*

Question 2: Does the title create curiosity? Does it make you want to know more about the book? *Yes, everyone loves checklists, and the author shows you how to use them to become more efficient with data and case studies to support it!*

Question 3: Does the title/subtitle imply value for the reader? Is there an implied promise or an answer to the reader's ultimate question, "What's in it for me?" What are the benefits to the reader? *The benefits are listed in his subtitle: "How to Get Things Done Right"!*

Question 4: Would a reader feel cool to be seen reading a book with that title? Readers have egos, and titles that people deem offensive or out-of-date and can therefore hinder sales. *Sure! It's a positive book on checklists, systems, and productivity!*

Question 5: Does the title help build the author's brand and enable the creation of complementary spin-off resources, such as online programs, consulting, coaching, seminars, and other types of curriculum for non-fiction authors? *He's a doctor, so this gives him more exposure than he would get in private practice, and yes, it does build his brand!*

So, this book gets a thumbs-up as well!

Malcolm Gladwell:

If you want to study a well-known author who is amazing at selecting bestselling titles, let's take a look at Malcolm Gladwell and dissect how all of his books are titled. Malcolm's books have sold over 5 million copies!

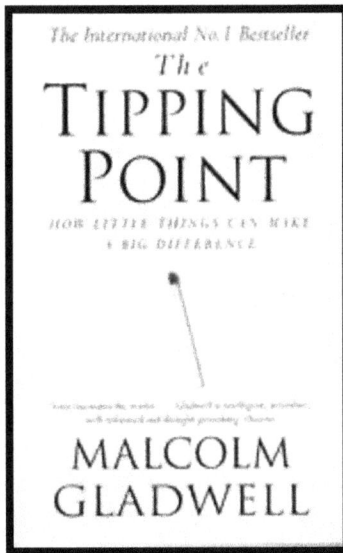

Here are some of the most popular ones you may have heard of:

- *The Tipping Point: How Little Things Can Make a Big Difference*

- *Blink: The Power of Thinking Without Thinking*

- *Outliers: The Story of Success*

- *David and Goliath: Underdogs, Misfits and the Art of Battling Giants*

- *What the Dog Saw: And Other Adventures*

So, let's break down how he titles his bestselling books so you can do the same:

- 1-3-word catchy, memorable titles

- Curiosity-building titles

- Subtitles that also evoke curiosity and give a glimpse into the benefits

- Short and sweet

The key is to start with an end in mind:

- Who are you writing to?

- Who do you serve?

- What do you offer?

- How will this book attract them?

Then, create a HOOK: You need a 3-5 word (ideally) main title that provokes curiosity or emotional responses!

Use the subtitle to give the promise, benefits, and an explanation of the book.

But don't be too wordy…keep it simple.

Interrupting the Marketing Noise

There is a lot of noise in the competitive world of marketing. So, how do you rise above that marketing noise?

In MJ DeMarco's book, "*The Millionaire Fastlane,*" the author says there are five ways to do this:

1) Polarize

2) Arouse Emotions

3) Be Risqué'

4) Encourage Interaction

5) Be UN-Conventional

The key is to GRAB people's attention with your title, subtitle, and cover! That's how you get them to read the book's preview, and if they like that, then they will hit the BUY button. It all starts with the title, subtitle, and cover. Be different and don't be afraid to stand out!

EXERCISE: Now that you know the recipe for a Bestselling title, I want you to come up with at least 10 title ideas for your book idea.

You can test them through your email list or on social media by creating a survey or contest where people can vote on them.

Let your followers help you out on this one. Another thing I recommend all authors do is to...

Keep a Title Journal

This may sound crazy, but I have a journal I keep close by me at home which I labeled as my "Title" journal. When title ideas come to me, which is almost daily, I write them down in my Title journal.

Many times, I'm reading a book and I see a phrase that I think would make a great title, so I add it to my Title journal.

Then, when I'm struggling to find a good book title, chapter title, etc., I can easily go to my handy Title journal and pick one out. I have hundreds of titles in this notebook.

Hopefully, this information will help you come up with some awesome killer titles!

CHAPTER 4

LAUNCH OR PERISH

"Without promotion, something terrible happens…Nothing!" ~ *P.T. Barnum*

A book launch is a designated time period (usually 1-5 days) in which you put all of your book marketing efforts to encourage readers to buy (or download) your book.

The ultimate goal of a book launch is to get the highest number of sales (downloads) in the shortest amount of time so your book will hit as many Amazon Bestseller lists as possible. This will increase your visibility exponentially and readers can now find you!

We will talk more about how to stay on bestseller lists, but the first goal is to reach the bestsellers list.

WHAT YOU SHOULD KNOW ABOUT AMAZON BESTSELLERS LISTS

Having your book on a Bestseller list = High Visibility!

Having visibility on Amazon and being on bestsellers lists is akin to getting your website to Page one of Google. It's not easy to do, but if you can do it, you will have much more success.

Why Is It Important to Be on The Bestsellers Lists?

Because bestsellers lists are the most searched lists on Amazon. When potential readers are searching for keywords on Amazon, don't you want your book to show up in the search results?

NOTE: Amazon does not automatically put books in the correct categories when published. You must research the bestsellers lists and categories, then submit a customer support ticket to have your book added to more categories.

How Many Bestseller Lists Are There?

It's estimated there are over 10,000 bestsellers lists on Amazon. Think of broad categories like: Nonfiction, Fiction, Business, Memoirs, or Biographies. For every broad category, there are dozens of subcategories. The goal is for your book to show up on as many bestsellers lists as possible to reach more readers.

How Do You Get Your Book on These Bestsellers Lists?

Do a book launch to get a high number of sales/downloads in a short period of time and your book will be on multiple bestsellers lists as long as you chose the right categories. To remain on the bestsellers list after the launch, you need consistent sales.

I mentioned this earlier, but I want to reiterate there are PAID bestsellers lists and FREE bestsellers lists. For my clients, I typically start with a 2-day FREE launch and then their books organically go over to the paid bestsellers list; this is a 2-stage or 2-step launch.

Why Give Away A Book During A Free Book Launch?

Unless you have a large email list or social media following, you will get a lot more exposure for your book doing a FREE bestseller launch. The difference could be possibly thousands of downloads on a FREE promotion vs. 100-500 downloads on a PAID promotion (book launch). Also, if you include a link for a free gift in your book, you may influence readers to join your email list. Moreover, you will you get additional reviews because more people will have your book.

What Happens When My Book Is on A Bestsellers List?

- You have visibility and potential readers can find your book.

- "Bestsellers lists" are highly searched because when people want to solve a problem, they look for books in those categories and bestsellers lists, which is good for you.

- Your book has been indexed by Amazon and is removed from obscurity.

- The mysterious Amazon Algorithm is triggered, and if you get enough downloads and sales, Amazon will start marketing your book! Wouldn't it be nice to have Amazon promoting your book on various lists, to their Prime members, and even take out Pay-Per-Click ads and Facebook ads for your book? Amazon does this for many authors when they get on the bestsellers list.

What Is the Amazon Algorithm?

There is a lot of talk about the Amazon algorithm, but no one really knows exactly what it is. Just like no one can tell you what the Google algorithm is for being on Page one of the search results for your keywords.

However, I can tell you that based on my extensive testing, research, and experience from doing over 250 book launches, I've determined that the following criteria most likely influences the Amazon Algorithm:

- Number of reviews (the more the better)
- Properly selected keywords
- Properly selected categories
- A book description containing keywords
- A title or subtitle with keywords, if possible
- Being on multiple bestsellers lists
- Being listed as a Hot New Release (to get on this list, you must do the book launch within 30 days of publishing your book)
- No errors in your book
- Beautiful cover

Once you are the #1 bestseller in your selected categories and your book is being downloaded and doing well, Amazon starts promoting your book in several different ways with its own internal marketing system.

I cannot guarantee that any book will stay a bestseller or do well forever (the market decides what it likes), however, I have many clients whose books have remained on these bestseller lists for months and years. Just be aware that you need to continue to market and promote your book after the book launch.

In addition to placing your book on a bestsellers list, Amazon will often promote your book on other popular lists, such as:

- New for You
- Recommendations
- Based on your Browsing History
- Frequently Bought Together
- Hot New Releases (you can only get on this list within 30 days of publishing your book).
- Customers who bought this item also bought…
- Movers and Shakers
- Top Rated
- What Other Items Do Customers Buy After Viewing this Item?
- AND MORE!

Remember, once your book becomes a #1 bestseller, you will hold that title for life!

You can add that bestseller title to your website, social media pages, book cover, and use this esteemed title to elevate your credibility, authority, impact, and income.

Some Things You Might Not Know:

- Amazon updates their bestsellers lists several times a day.

- There can be 1 to 100 books on each bestsellers list.

- There are over 10,000 categories on Amazon. 95% of authors choose the wrong categories when publishing their book which means that their book is hidden from people who are looking for those types of books.

- Amazon allows you to choose only two broad categories when self-publishing on Amazon KDP. However, if you want your book to be a bestseller, you will have to research to find additional subcategories. Then, send a customer support ticket to KDP to have your book added to those additional categories.

- You can become a bestseller on the FREE bestsellers list initially. However, ultimately, you want your book to be on the PAID bestsellers list.

- If you make your book exclusive to Amazon for 90 days through their "Kindle Select" program, you can use their promotional tools and offer your book for free for up to five days, every 90 days.

- It's important that before the book launch is scheduled that you have the highest quality book cover and a magnetic book description that converts browsers into buyers!

I have created a program and system that I use for my launches, but the above information gives you an overview of what to do when launching your books.

PRIOR TO THE LAUNCH:

- Make sure your book has five reviews before you hire book promoters. Note, I initially price the eBook at $.99 so I can easily get sales and reviews. In other words, it's easier to ask people to buy your eBook at $.99 to get reviews than it would be at a higher price.

- Have a compelling book description that piques the reader's interest, coupled with a strong call to action that will make readers want to purchase your book.

- Select the best keywords for your book by doing keyword research using Publisher Rocket.

- Email KDP customer support to add your book to up to a total of 10 categories. This way, your book can hit as many bestsellers lists as possible. Choose categories that are less competitive so your book can hit the top of the bestsellers lists.

PREPARING FOR THE LAUNCH

- Schedule your book launch 10-14 days in advance ideally.

- Hire 5-10 promoters to promote your book during your designated launch. I do 2-day launches for my clients to the FREE bestsellers lists and a 1-day launch for my own books to the PAID bestsellers lists at $.99. *Note*:

Some promoters only accept promotions for *free books*, and some only accept *paid promotions*. The promoters I use for free and paid launches are listed in the Resources section of this book.

- Set up social media posts with a service like Hootsuite so that you are promoting your book to all of your social media sites on book launch day(s). I post on Twitter hourly and Facebook and LinkedIn a few times on book launch days.

- If you have an email list, send out an email to your list(s) on book launch day(s) first thing in the morning.

WHAT TO DO ON BOOK LAUNCH DAY:

- Amazon updates these bestsellers lists at least a few times a day. I recommend checking your book's rankings in the late afternoon and evening on book launch day to allow Amazon time to update the lists and sales rankings.

- Amazon will ONLY show the top three bestseller lists on your Amazon product/book page. However, your book will most likely be on an additional 10-20 bestsellers lists (if you selected the right categories). Amazon will show your book in the subcategories you chose, but make sure you check the main categories as well. For example, if you selected the category of Small Business Franchise, it would show up as *Kindle eBooks>Business & Money>Entrepreneurship & Small Business>Franchises*. On your product page, Amazon will simply show your book as #1 in the *Franchises* category. Check to see if your book is on these other bestsellers lists for *Business & Money* and *Entrepreneurship & Small Business.*

- Click on the bestseller list links to take screenshots of your book. If you don't see your book listed, make sure you are viewing the right list (paid vs. free). Go to all the categories you put your book in and get screenshots of all those bestseller lists, especially those in which you hit #1.

- Create a marketing collage using a free service like PicMonkey or Canva and share your bestseller results on social media. You can view sample collages I've created for my clients at: https://bestsellingauthorprogram.com/ graduates/

WHAT TO DO AFTER THE LAUNCH

- Continue to market your book once you are a #1 Amazon Bestselling Author. Marketing a book is not a one-and-done event.

- Immediately set up Amazon Ads with at least 500–1,000 keywords after the book launch. This is critical to the success of your book following the launch.

- Add the bestseller logo to your book cover and resubmit to Amazon (it can take 12-48 hours for approval).

- Immediately set up media interviews (podcasts and radio shows) once you become a bestselling author. I use a paid service to get booked on top podcast shows.

- If you did the 2-day free launch, and your book is not at the top of the paid bestsellers list within a week or so, then do a paid promotion to bump your book up even higher on the bestsellers lists.

- BookBub is great book promotion service for authors. You should apply for a *Featured Deal* to get in front of millions of book readers. Just know that you must wait 90 days after doing a free or discounted book launch before submitting your book.

- If you don't get accepted for a *Featured Deal* on BookBub, you can run BookBub ads, which don't require the in-depth editorial review that a *Featured Deal* requires.

- If you don't get accepted by BookBub.com, then try Ereadernewstoday.com or RobinReads.com.

- I recommend hiring book promoters every 60-90 days to maintain your position on these bestsellers lists.

- Put 3D mock-ups of your book cover and links to your bestselling book on the home page of your website (if you have one.)

- Add something about your book to your autoresponder email series so that you are continually marketing your book to your list.

I teach this system to my students and use it for my own book launches, so it is a proven system.

I recently did a paid book launch for one of my books priced at $.99. I hit over a dozen bestsellers lists and reached #1 in four of those bestseller lists! I had over 400 sales coming off the $.99 2-day launch. I increased the price to $2.99 as soon as the 2-day launch was over. Because I have so many books, I can stay on top of the paid bestsellers lists with books priced at $2.99. If you notice your book rankings dropping suddenly, leave it at $.99 until it stabilizes on the paid bestsellers list and your Amazon Ads gain more traction.

Once my books are selling consistently, I usually increase the eBook price to $3.99. You can test different price points for your own books.

What About Print Books?

I am only talking about kindle eBook pricing here because the launch isn't for your print book. I usually price my print books at $14.97, and Amazon pays me 60% of royalties after the cost of printing (this is what's known as print-on-demand), so I typically earn a little over $6 for each print book sold. If someone buys my print book from a third party like Barnes & Noble, which goes through Amazon's expanded distribution, the royalties are lower at 40% minus the printing costs.

When you are doing a FREE or PAID eBook launch, you will most likely sell some print books organically. I always publish the eBook and paperback at the same time.

It's essential that you do a proper book launch.

Don't make the mistake many authors make by thinking readers will magically find your book after you hit the "publish" button from your Amazon KDP account.

I can tell you, with 100% certainty that I don't see the increase of my monthly sales for my book until I do the book launch because it is basically invisible on Amazon without a bestseller launch.

DO NOT SKIP THIS STEP!

CHAPTER 5

THE SECRET TO STAYING A BESTSELLER

I wish I could tell you that book marketing was a one-and-done event. Unfortunately, it doesn't work this way.

Once you launch your book to the top of the paid bestseller list, there are 20 action steps you can take to keep your book on the bestsellers lists:

At the very least, strive to do these top three action steps after your launch:

1. **Amazon Ads** - See Resources at the end of this book for a paid service to manage your ads.

2. **Media Interviews** – Get yourself booked on popular podcasts and/or radio shows. I have one client who has done over 600 interviews, and her book is still at the top of the bestsellers list, paying her mortgage, seven years after the launch!

3. **Hire Promoters** – After you do your first book launch, do them every 90 days and also try to get a **Book Bub Promotion.**

I have included a *MARKETING TIPS CHECKLIST* in this book to help you.

The goal is to spend 1-2 hours per week marketing your book, then another 1-2 hours a week writing your next book!

Book marketing is not a one-and-done event. It requires constant ACTION on your part.

If you're not getting the results you want or your book is slipping off the bestsellers list, more ACTION is needed on your part. You worked hard at becoming an Amazon Bestselling Author, and now it's time for you to work hard at "staying" on the Amazon Bestsellers lists and increasing your income.

It's do-able if you follow the "slow and steady wins the race" form of marketing instead of the "set-it and forget-it" marketing that many authors tend to do.

20 WAYS TO KEEP YOUR BOOK ON THE BESTSELLERS LIST

1. SET UP AMAZON ADS

Running Amazon ads is the #1 way to bring MORE visibility and MORE sales to your book.

After your launch, I recommend you speak with Alex (see the Resources section for his contact information), who can set up and manage your Amazon ads. Of course, you can do it yourself, but there is a learning curve to becoming proficient and understanding the Amazon Ads platform. Alex handles all of my ads currently.

If you want to learn how to do Amazon Ads yourself, Marc Reklau and I have created an additional paid training ($197). Marc is a 10x #1 bestselling author and used Amazon Ads to take his books from making under $1k per month to $25k+ per month in royalties.

You can learn more about and sign up for the training at:

https://bestsellingauthorprogram.com/amazon-ads-training

I highly recommend this advanced training. Many of my clients have taken what they learned in this training and saw results and sales right away!

10 REASONS TO RUN AMAZON ADS

1. Low cost in comparison to Facebook ads and in my opinion (having done both), are an easier platform to navigate than Facebook ads.

2. They have a great ROI once you get the ads working.

3. This isn't guesswork. Ads are based on keywords that people are searching for on Amazon.

4. Amazon has a secret algorithm for books, and I believe that when an author is paying for ads, Amazon includes that in their algorithm and promotes the author's book even more.

5. You can get started with a budget as low as $5 or $10 a day.

6. Ads get your book in front of potential readers who would not normally see it.

7. You want to be ubiquitous and be seen in front of thousands of people, and you do that by having thousands of keywords working for you.

8. Amazon ads are like having a salesperson working for your book 24/7.

9. You can use software like Publisher Rocket to find thousands of keywords to set up your first ad easily.

10. I have clients that double their sales with Amazon ads.

2. GET BOOKED ON AT LEAST ONE PODCAST OR RADIO SHOW EVERY WEEK OR EVERY MONTH TO DRIVE BOOK SALES

One of my very first clients, Nancy Hartwell, has now done over 600 interviews since launching her book in 2013. And she's still at the top of the bestsellers list!

Although Nancy wrote a "fiction" book, she is now seen as an expert on *Human Slave Trafficking*, which is the topic of that fiction book.

A great benefit of doing interviews is that you become the *expert* on a topic, and as a former newspaper reporter, I can tell you the media is always on the hunt for good stories!

You may not LOVE doing radio interviews, but if you LOVE money and want people to learn about you (and your book), then I suggest you step out of your comfort zones and start doing radio interviews.

One of my authors told me that if he was a #1 bestseller, CNN said they would have him on the show! So, believe me, being a bestselling author has many benefits, and the media is interested in hearing from you!

Your goal should be one podcast or radio interview per week or, at a minimum, per month. See the Resources section at the end of this book for a recommendation on a great company that can book you on top podcasts.

3. SIGN UP AT HARO – HELP A REPORTER OUT

From *The New York Times*, to ABC News, to HuffingtonPost.com and everyone in between, nearly 30,000 members of the media have quoted HARO sources in their stories. Everyone's an expert at something. Sharing your expertise may land you that big media opportunity you've been seeking.

How it Works. Sign up for a FREE account. Scan the emails, and if you're knowledgeable about any of the topics, reply to the reporter directly through the anonymous @helpareporter.net email address provided at the beginning of the query.

That's it!

I like how the emails are categorized, such as business and finance, high tech, etc. You can choose the topics for which you want to receive emails.

Read the inquiries daily and apply to those that match your expertise!

To learn more about HARO, visit www.helpareporter.com.

First, read the following article that contains tips and templates for submitting articles:

www.tckpublishing.com/how-to-use-haro-to-get-free-publicity

4. HIRE PAID BOOK PROMOTERS

After the FREE 2-Day Launch, I recommend keeping your eBook priced at $.99 for 1-4 weeks so that it will stabilize on the paid bestsellers list. Some authors leave their books at $.99 permanently. It depends your goals.

NOTE: When your eBook is priced between $2.99 and $9.99, you earn 70% royalties from Amazon. If the eBook is priced below $2.99 or above $9.99, then you only earn 35% royalties.

So, you're probably wondering why you should leave your eBook at $.99.

The goal after the FREE 2-day launch is to get your book ranked as high as possible on the PAID Bestsellers list so you have visibility and readers can find your book.

If you've done the work, your book will be set up in the BEST CATEGORIES. You can change your categories any time after the launch if you find your book is falling off the bestsellers list. Sometimes, the competition increases after a launch and you may need to find new categories in which your book can rank high.

Here's more about the $.99 post-launch strategy:

When I do a book launch for my clients, I hire several book promoters, which means your book is in the virtual world on many different websites and Facebook groups. Readers will still find your book in those places and click on the link after the FREE launch is over. Although the FREE promotion is over, if you leave it at $.99, visitors will likely still purchase your book. This is how giving away a FREE eBook converts to sales after the 2-day free launch!

5. SUBMIT YOUR BOOK TO BOOKBUB – THE INTERNET'S LARGEST BOOK PROMOTER!

BookBub is the #1 service for publishers and authors looking to reach new readers through limited-time eBook deals. BookBub features free and deeply discounted eBook deals in a daily targeted email and on their website, reaching millions of readers every day.

90 days after your FREE Promotion, submit your book to be promoted by BookBub! Add an event to your calendar to remind you.

Note: This is NOT a FREE service – there is a fee for this service.

Here is a description from their website:

Because BookBub's content is curated, our partners can be confident they're reaching engaged readers. BookBub members choose the genres they want to receive, and our team of editorial experts' hand-selects each book we feature from our pool of submissions. Ensuring that our members only receive top-quality content in categories they like keeps members coming back to BookBub again and again to discover new books and authors.

Featuring your promotion with BookBub can help drive sales for backlist titles, boost a book up the bestseller lists, or introduce our audience of passionate power readers to their next favorite series.

The number of subscribers BookBub has on various lists is included on this page which they update regularly: www.bookbub.com/partners/pricing (You can also see pricing on that page.)

Here are some links for you:

- https://www.bookbub.com/partners/how-it-works
- https://www.bookbub.com/partners/submission-tips
- https://bookbub.desk.com/?b_id=4259 (FAQs)

Many successful authors have promotions going for their books at all times. Those with several books often have one or two promotions running concurrently.

6. DO A "COUNTDOWN DEAL" ON AMAZON

Amazon KDP (Kindle Direct Publishing) offers two main pro-motion tools that are FREE promotions in which Amazon gives you five days to promote your book every 90 days at no cost.

Countdown deals are only permitted one time every 90 days.

Amazon won't allow you to schedule one of these deals until your book has been in the KDP program for at least 30 days.

Also, your book must be priced between $2.99 and $24.99, and you must offer at least $1 off the regular price. NOTE: You can't change the book's price 30 days prior to the Countdown deal and 14 days after the Countdown deal.

Schedule your Countdown deals approximately 30 days after your big launch and promotion, so schedule it on your calendar NOW. This is an excellent way to get more readers for your book and boost your rankings!

To set up a Countdown deal, log in to your Amazon KDP account at kdp.amazon.com and then click on the "Bookshelf" link (see image below). Click on the promotions tab next to the book you want to set up.

The Countdown deal can last a minimum of one hour to a maximum of seven days.

You can earn 70% royalties if your book is priced below $2.99 during the Countdown deal! As you know, you normally only earn 35% royalties if your book is priced below $2.99 and above $9.99. So, if you do a Countdown deal for seven days for $.99 or $1.99, you will earn 70% royalties instead of the typical 35% royalties for those price points.

To read more about Amazon Countdown deals, visit:

https://kdp.amazon.com/en_US/help/topic/G201293780

7. DO ANOTHER "FREE" PROMOTION

You are given five FREE promotion days when you sign up to be in the Amazon KDP Select program (you agreed to sell your book *exclusively* on Amazon for 90 days).

If you only used two of those FREE days during your launch, you still have three FREE promotion days remaining.

So, you can do another FREE promotion if you like.

NOTE: If you have large email list, you do NOT need to do FREE promotions. You can do a discounted promotion of your eBook at $.99. Just know that some promoters you hire only do free and some only do paid, so pay close attention.

8. BUILD YOUR EMAIL LIST AND SET-UP AUTORESPONDERS

THE MONEY IS IN THE LIST! I'd rather have a new sign up on my email list than a sale on Amazon because I can nurture the new subscriber. Amazon doesn't share emails or reader contact information with authors.

If you have a website, you should be building your email list. If you publish additional books, then you can easily communicate with your new readers.

Ways to Build Your Email List

1. Start a **PUBLIC FACEBOOK GROUP** and start inviting people to join. Make the group enticing and post in the group DAILY adding value (not just saying, "Buy my book"). It's about being engaged. People will see what you're doing and that you are an expert on your topic, and you can turn these leads into subscribers and clients! Here are some large Facebook groups (including some of my client's groups) that you can look at for an example:

   - **Heart Centered, Soul Driven Entrepreneurs -** www.facebook.com/groups/714631208567627/ *Tash has 34,000+ members in this group!

   - **The Financially Free Entrepreneur:** www.facebook.com/groups/1605968559619362/ *Over 5,000 members

   - **The Super Attractor book group by Gabby Bernstein has over 9,000 members**: www.facebook.com/groups/660132307709837/

2. Offer a **FREE GIFT (LEAD MAGNET)** on your website (or if you don't have a website just use www.leadpages.net or Click Funnels) and promote that with paid Facebook Ads and on social media. Your FREE Gift should be something

that your ideal client wants (solves a BIG problem for them) and is willing to pay for (but you're giving it away for FREE)!

3. Use a **POP-UP FORM ON YOUR WEBSITE** and watch subscriber rates soar! I use www.popupdomination.com, and the plans start at $9 per month.

4. Become a **CONTRIBUTING WRITER** on big sites like Huffington Post, Mind, Body, Green, or Forbes, and you will gain followers from there.

5. Do a **JOINT VENTURE** with someone who has a complementary program to what you offer and split the proceeds with them. This will grow your email list exponentially if your partner has a big email list.

6. Run **FACEBOOK ADS** and select interest groups that correspond with your topic/genre.

7. Do an **AUTOMATED WEBINAR** on your topic. **THIS IS MY FAVORITE** You can run paid Facebook ads to your automated webinar. You can sell a product at the end OR sign them up for a strategy session. This is a great way to build an email list quickly, but make sure your autoresponders are set up so you can follow up with the new subscriber frequently. I used this method to grow my email list and get new clients for my Amazon Bestseller program for years.

8. Be a **GUEST ON RADIO SHOWS AND PODCASTS** – We already talked about this, but I wanted to mention it's a good idea offer your free gift during the interview. You can mention your book, of course, but it's a good idea to capture listener's email and have them on your list so that you can continue to market to them.

9. **DO A GIVEAWAY**! This is a great way to build your email list fast. Here is an example of someone who did a giveaway and collected *187,991 email subscribers* using King Sumo: https://kingsumo.com/apps/giveaways/

10. Follow this **30-DAY ROADMAP TO GROW YOUR EMAIL LIST**: https://sumo.com/stories/grow-email-list

NEXT, add your book to your email Autoresponders. If you have a website/blog and you are giving a FREE gift away to build your email list (which you absolutely should be doing), then you should add new autoresponders at the beginning of your funnel to send when someone signs up for your list!

You can add as many messages as you like, just spread them out. Include quotes from your book or tips, ideas, and strategies, and then link to your book.

MJ DeMarco does this very well with his book, "**The Millionaire Fastlane**," which has been on the bestsellers list for years.

You can sign up for his list here to see what I am talking about: http://www.themillionairefastlane.com/

If you like what he's doing, then model your autoresponders the same way.

To be successful, you have to PROMOTE your book in multiple ways.

9. HOST OR BE A CONTRIBUTOR ON A VIRTUAL SUMMIT

Each summit has a theme, and the summit's host interviews experts on that topic and then sells access to the information presented. All of the summit participants promote it to their email list, so it's a great way to build your list.

Whether you want to host your own summit or be a featured expert, it is a great way for you and your book to get more exposure.

Here's an example of a summit:

https://womeninpublishingsummit.com/

There are also books written on how to create summits for authors, such as this one by fellow author friend of mine, Ray Brehm:

https://www.amazon.com/gp/product/B08DM9VN6J/

10. HAVE A SPEAKER ONE SHEET

If you want to be a guest on radio shows or podcasts, you should have a Speaker One Sheet. Include your bio, a description of your latest book, suggested topics, and suggested questions. Here is a sample of my latest Speaker One Sheet:

MICHELLE KULP

Michelle Kulp is a Book Launch Expert, Publishing Specialist, and 10x #1 Bestselling Author. Since 2012, she has been teaching entrepreneurs, consultants, coaches, and thought leaders how to elevate their expertise, attract their ideal clients, and increase their income and opportunities — with a Bestselling Book! To date, Michelle has launched over 250 books for clients through her program.

Michelle's Amazon Bestseller program is a one-stop shop for authors who don't have the knowledge, expertise, desire or skill-set to publish and market their own books. Michelle takes her 15 years of online experience and 7 years as a working author to provide a much-needed service to experts who want to use a book to build their business and credibility.

28 Books to $100K

In a survey done by Written Word Media, it was discovered that "$100Kers" had an average of **28 books in their catalog.** They also found that 80% of authors make less than $6,000 per year, which is not a livable income.

Michelle decided she would test this "theory" and has been writing one book per month since January 2020. In just 9 short months, she has created $2,300 per month in passive income using this system and is on target to pay all of her living expenses with her royalties in the next six months with the option to retire early.

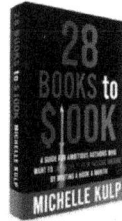

Suggested Topics

- Creating Passive Income with Writing
- Writing One Book Per Month
- Digital Retirement (Wealth With Words)
- Becoming a #1 Bestselling Author for the Sake of Visibility
- Leveraging Your Book to Build Your Business and Brand

Suggested Questions

- What can a writer do to stand out amongst so much competition?
- How can a book be utilized to help build an entrepreneur's business and brand?
- How can you make 6-figures by writing one book per month?
- How can an author reverse engineer the profit into their book?

BESTSELLING *Author* PROGRAM

f /MICHELLE.BACHTELER.KULP   @6FIGUREWOMAN   in /MICHELLE-KULP

11. BLOG ABOUT YOUR TOPIC USING KEYWORDS/SEO IN YOUR POSTS AND LINK TO YOUR BOOK

A blog post can give readers searching for information about your topic some answers to their problem, and they can connect with you and subscribe to your email list!

When you blog, include a link for readers to purchase your book and get more book sales.

The image of your book should be prominent on your website's home page and should link directly to your Amazon sales page.

Start blogging 1-4x per month about your topic! I have done this in the past and received a lot of traffic from Google because I had "new" fresh content. Google loves fresh content and doesn't like "stagnant" sites.

Don't blog just a few paragraphs of basic information people can find anywhere on the internet; blog like you were writing for the Huffington Post! I typically spend 1-2 hours writing my blog posts.

As soon as I hit "publish" for my blog post, I have an "automated blog broadcast" set up in my Aweber account, so it goes out to my entire list! You can do this manually if you don't have that set up, but I highly recommend automating it.

Also, after I hit "publish" on my blog post and have a link to it, I write some benefit-driven reasons WHY they should read the blog post! Then, I post that blog post in the following places:

- My personal Facebook page
- My 10 private Facebook groups
- Twitter
- LinkedIn
- Pinterest

When you are writing blog posts, make sure that you are using a keyword tool to select the most searched keywords in your genre, so your blog post is optimized for search engines to find.

12. BE A GUEST BLOGGER

As a guest blogger, you can tap into other followers of that blog and its subscriber list. This is a great way to get more signups for your email list and exposure for your book.

Read this article for a list of guest posting sites (2019):

https://www.outreachmama.com/guest-posting-sites/

13. OFFER A SPECIAL COUPON CODE IN YOUR BOOK

If you are selling a program like an online course or a coaching program on the backend of your book, you can include a discount for your book's readers at the end of the book.

For example, let's say I am selling an online course for $997 but on my sales page, I offer a 50% discount to anyone who purchases my book from Amazon and then emails me the code.

This incentivizes visitors to your site to purchase your book on Amazon, and you also get a new student for your online course! Win/Win

In fact, you might want to create an online course just so you can use this strategy!

Offer a coupon code and you will increase your book sales and make money on the backend!

14. LISTEN TO STEVE SCOTT'S INTERVIEW. STEVE MAKES $40K PER MONTH WITH HIS BOOKS

Steve Scott (who writes under the name "S.J. Scott" on Amazon) did an interview with James Altucher titled, "How to Go from $0-$40,000 a Month Writing from Home." I highly encourage you to listen to the interview.

In 2012, Steve started publishing books on Amazon KDP, and now with 42+ books published, he is making five figures per month! This story will inspire you as this is a great way to create passive income and multiple streams of income.

Here is the link to the Steve Scott interview:

http://www.jamesaltucher.com/2014/07/ep-23-go-0-40000-month-writing-home/

15. READ NEGATIVE REVIEWS ON AMAZON AND MAKE ADJUSTMENTS

The great thing about publishing on Amazon's KDP platform is that you can make changes to your book one day and re-publish your book that very same day!

One of my clients continues to improve her book by making adjustments after reading negative reviews on Amazon.

Unfortunately, many of the negative reviews are without merit (just a subjective opinion of her book), but there are a few that have merit (i.e., constructive criticism).

Read through your reviews, especially the negative ones, and see if there are constructive comments. Maybe there are problems with punctuation, grammar, and spelling, or the reader might have felt like something was "missing" from the book. That could be an opportunity for you to add a new chapter or section to make the book even better (especially if it's a non-fiction book). Or you might consider writing a sequel or follow up book to include what readers say is lacking.

The important point here is to view each negative review as an opportunity to find out what the readers want and use that information to improve the quality of your book (or to write your next book)!

Sometimes after reading the reviews, you might be inspired to write a new book about topics your current book didn't cover.

16. WRITE ANOTHER BOOK

If you were playing the lottery, you wouldn't just buy one lottery ticket, right? Well, maybe you would. But if you wanted to increase your odds of winning, then you would buy lots of tickets.

When it comes to making money with books, you increase your odds of making money by having more books to sell. You never know which book will be a big hit and take off, just like a songwriter can't predict which song will take off. The market decides what they like and want.

When you write and publish multiple books on Amazon, you start getting reader loyalty and reader transference, which means if they like one of your books, they will often buy other books by you.

Don't stop with one book as you may be disappointed at the amount of income it generates. Once you have three books in the same genre, then you have a series and can sell it as a box set, which will do well on Amazon because readers can purchase all three books at once for a discounted price. People love them!

17. ADD AN EMAIL SIGNATURE WITH A LINK TO YOUR FREE GIFT ON YOUR WEBSITE TO BUILD YOUR EMAIL LIST OR TO YOUR BOOK

This is a simple and easy way to grow your following.

Below is a screenshot of my current email signature:

```
New Message                                        —  ⤢  ✕

  To

  From  Michelle Kulp <michelle.kulp@gmail.com>  ▾          Cc  Bcc

  Subject


  ***********************
  Michelle Kulp
  WANTED:  #1 Bestselling Authors
  Sign up to have a FREE Book Discovery Session with me at:
  www.bestsellingauthorprogram.com
```

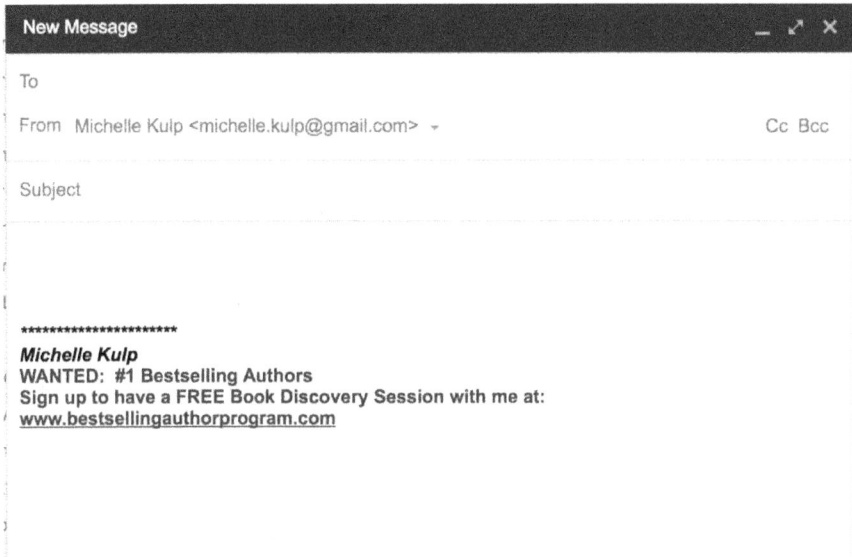

18. TAKE MARK DAWSON'S "ADS FOR AUTHORS" PROGRAM WHEN IT OPENS UP

Mark Dawson is an attorney from the UK, who now makes seven figures with his books and does this full-time. Mark knows from experience the path to making high royalties from books!

During our Amazon Ads training, Marc Reklau, mentioned that he used Dawson's system and took his books from making under $1k per month on Amazon to over $25k per month now.

19. PURCHASE PUBLISHER ROCKET

During our Amazon Ads training, Marc and I talk about Publisher Rocket, which is the tool we both use to for finding keywords and for setting up Amazon ads.

I mentioned this earlier and am repeating it here because this tool has saved us hundreds of hours manually searching for keywords on Amazon, and we highly recommend it!

20. SET UP YOUR AUTHOR CENTRAL PAGE

An author central page is a bio page on Amazon where people can follow you. To get it set up you will upload a photo, write a bio, and if you want to build your list, then in the description, tell readers to visit your website to get your FREE Gift and put in the link on your bio page. Include the link to your Amazon Author Central page in your blog, videos, social media accounts, and more!

This is very important, so if you haven't done this, I want you to do it right now: https://authorcentral.amazon.com/

If you have more than one book published (and hopefully that is your goal), all of your books will show up on your Author Central page.

You can also add your blog to your Author Central page so your blog posts will appear.

Book marketing is not a one-and-done event. It requires constant activity on your part.

The key is to spend 1-2 hours a week marketing your book and 1-2 hours a week writing your next book!

I've seen a lot of people pay $10,000 to $20,000 for PR professionals to market their book with very poor results.

I recommend doing it the old-fashioned way (yourself) until you're so famous that you don't need to do any marketing!

Below is a *Book Marketing Checklist* which will help you stay organized.

I also recommend keeping track of your book's stats, so you know what marketing efforts are working and what's not working.

MARKETING CHECKLIST:

- ☐ Run Amazon Ads (an absolute MUST)
- ☐ Get booked on at least one podcast and/or radio show every WEEK or every MONTH!
- ☐ Use Paid Book Promoters immediately following the 2-day free launch and promote your book at $.99 to get to the top of the Paid Bestsellers List
- ☐ Submit your book to "Book Bub" for a featured deal 90-day after your promotion/book launch
- ☐ Do a "Countdown Deal" on Amazon every 90 days
- ☐ Do a "Free" or "Paid" promotion every 90 days
- ☐ Build your email list with the *Top 10 Ways to Grow an Email List*
- ☐ Create autoresponders on your email list
- ☐ Sign Up at HARO – Help A Reporter Out

- ☐ Host a Summit
- ☐ Get an Author website (If you don't have one or at least have a landing page, use the tools: Leadpages or ClickFunnels)
- ☐ Blog about your topic and link to your book on Amazon
- ☐ Add your book to your autoresponder series and to your home page
- ☐ Purchase Publisher Rocket
- ☐ Listen to Steve Scott's interview and find out how he makes $40k a month on his books: www.jamesaltucher.com/2014/07/ep-23-go-0-40000-month-writing-home/
- ☐ Make sure your Author Central Page is set up
- ☐ Become a Guest Blogger
- ☐ Offer a special coupon code at the end of your book for follow-up programs and/or services
- ☐ Read negative reviews on Amazon and adjust your book if needed
- ☐ Write a Book a Month and join my free Facebook group: www.facebook.com/groups/28BooksTo100K
- ☐ Add an Email signature with a call to action
- ☐ Listen to my interview with Marc Guberti on making money with your book that you can listen to here: http://marcguberti.com/2019/05/e345-becoming-a-bestselling-author-is-the-key-to-becoming-a-highly-paid-authority-in-your-space-with-michelle-kulp/

CHAPTER 6

THE BESTSELLER CHECKLIST

This goal isn't just to quickly write and publish a book; the goal is to put out a high-quality book that will be launched to the bestsellers list and remain on there for a long time. To help do this, I have created a *Bestseller Checklist* for you.

Here's an overview of the Bestseller Checklist:

- ☐ Start with the End
- ☐ Pound the Payoff
- ☐ The Snowflake Hook
- ☐ Attached at the Hip
- ☐ Cover Judgement
- ☐ Ramp Up Reviews
- ☐ The Preview Presell
- ☐ The Synopsis Cliffhanger
- ☐ Know Your Quick Pitch
- ☐ Launch Like a Pro

Each item on the checklist is described below. Think of these items as creating a solid foundation for your book.

1. START WITH THE END

First, pick your profit path strategy. The four biggest authority profit engines from a bestselling book are:

1. Speaking Engagements

2. High-Ticket Coaching

3. Digital Courses

4. Live Events

Many authors earn 6-7 figures on the backend of their books. Think beyond the book—your book is only the beginning. It's often the first introduction people have to you, and it effortlessly turns a cold lead into a warm lead. When someone reads your book and needs help implementing the strategies you presented, that's your opportunity to help them while you increase the profits from your book. Win-Win!

2. POUND THE PAYOFF

What's in it for them? If your book is all about you, readers will quickly lose interest. Make sure your title, subtitle, and especially your book description shows the potential reader the IMMENSE benefits they will receive from reading your book.

3. THE SNOWFLAKE HOOK

No two snowflakes are the same. You must create a book that has NOT been written before. Here are some ideas (with actual book titles as examples):

- **Change the Perspective**: *Public Speaking for People Who Hate Public Speaking*

- **Shock Factor**: *The Subtle Art of Not Giving a F*ck*

- **Create a New Process/Method/System**: *Habit Stacking: 127 Small Changes to Improve Your Health, Wealth and Happiness*

- **Make the Complicated Simple**: *The Index Card: Why Personal Finance Doesn't Have to Be Complicated*

- **Against the Norm**: *The 30-Hour Day: Develop Achiever's Mindset and Habits*

- **Contrary Messaging** – *The Obstacle is the Way*

- **Solve a Million Dollar Problem**: *Profit First: Transform Your Business from a Cash-Eating Monster to a Money-Making Machine*

- **Mimic the Classics** – *Write and Grow Rich*

A good hook grabs the reader's attention and piques interest! Think outside the box.

4. ATTACHED AT THE HIP

Authors need to be thinking about lifetime followers, NOT only one-time readers. Offer the reader a high-value lead magnet at the beginning of your book and gain a lifetime follower on your email list. Also, start a Facebook group for your readers and include an invitation to join in your book. Then, you can develop a relationship with them inside your private group! And, if you happen to sell something on the backend, these readers and followers may become clients!

5. COVER JUDGEMENT

Readers do judge books by their cover, so make sure your cover is professional, appealing, and attractive to your target audience.

- Pay a professional.
- Do a Design contest on platforms like 99designs.
- Take polls and surveys.
- Learn what your ideal reader likes.

I have a professional designer for all of my books, and I never skimp in this area.

6. RAMP UP REVIEWS

Good reviews sell books, bad reviews block sales. Getting reviews isn't easy, so put together a private Facebook group (aka your "Street Team") and gather your fans who will be the first to read your book when it comes out and are willing to write a review.

You can also use a free service like www.booksprout.co

7. THE PREVIEW PRESELL

Put your best foot forward. Amazon has a "Look Inside" feature also known as the "preview" that allows people considering purchasing a book to view 10% of the eBook's content. Make it Count! Don't fill it with Acknowledgements or lengthy disclaimers. Move that material to the back of the book. Put your best material in the front of your book!

8. THE SYNOPSIS CLIFFHANGER

Most book descriptions are poorly written because they contain dry facts and give away the contents of the book. Your book description should pique the readers' curiosity and leave them anxious to learn more. The three parts to a great book description are: 1) Identify the problem; 2) Hint at the possible solutions; 3) State why your book is the solution.

9. KNOW YOUR QUICK PITCH

"You know how _____ (problem)? Well, my book [shows/helps/does] _____ (solves problem), so they _____(benefit)." Fill in the blanks with your book.

Example: Quick Pitch for the book "How to Make People Like You in 90 Seconds or Less."

Quick Pitch: You know how some people have trouble connecting with others? Well, my book shows you how to do it naturally and easily... so you can be confident and get more out of life.

Knowing your Quick Pitch helps you quickly and easily explain your book to others.

10. LAUNCH LIKE A PRO

A book launch aims to get to the top of the Bestsellers list and go from being invisible to visible. As you know, bestseller lists are the most searched lists on Amazon. Once you are on a Bestsellers list, Amazon often promotes your book to its thousands of customers! There are several types of launches you can do depending on your goals with your book. For example, you can do free or paid launches, and you can do them for 1-5 days.

****

There you have it! The *Bestseller Checklist* will help you have a well-thought-out book instead of a hasty book that doesn't sell. The goal is to have long term sales, not just fast, easy sales when we launch.

CHAPTER 7

WHY YOU SHOULD WRITE
MORE THAN ONE BOOK

Your odds of winning the lottery increase if you buy more tickets. If you want to increase your profits from your book sales, you must write more books.

Since January 2020, I've been writing a book a month, and my income has increased 10x!

I started with a couple hundred dollars in royalties, and now I'm earning over $2,300 per month after nine months. I've also learned that 20% of my books make 80% of my income.

Guess what?

No one has a crystal ball to tell you which books are going to take off. I write every book with passion, heart and love, but I have no idea (even with all the keyword research I do) which books will strike a chord with people and ultimately take off.

I also believe that if you write books in one or two genres, then you'll become the go-to expert and authority in that genre.

Additionally, you can take three or more of your books and put them in a "box set" and create even more income selling your box sets.

My top-selling book right now is *How to Find Your Passion*. When readers are browsing on Amazon, a message will appear saying, "Customers who purchased this book also purchased" and then it shows the titles of my other two books:

Quit Your Job and Follow Your Dreams

Work from Home and Make 6 Figures

I plan to bundle these three books together soon and sell them as a box set.

It's Easier to Attract Readers for Your Books If You Can "Dominate" a Category or Two

Right now, I have six books on the "Women and Business" bestsellers list. I also have a few books on the career bestsellers lists.

Dominating categories increases the odds of readers finding your other books. You want to become ubiquitous on Amazon for your categories and niche'.

I called a client the other day who published two books on the law of attraction. I see him creating new content on YouTube every day, and it's phenomenal. I asked him if he was making any money from that content, and he is not.

Once I told him about my book a month program with my 28 books to $100K, he was super excited. This client can repurpose the content in those videos and write a book a month. By doing this, he will increase his income by 10x and attract new readers.

YouTube is great if you are making money from other people running ads on your videos, but he was not doing that. Now, he has a profit path for his content by repurposing it and writing a book a month.

We are starting with his first book next month!

Think of topics in which you are an expert in and want to write about. How could you break down that topic into multiple books?

MEET ALEX BERENSON WHO WRITES SHORT BOOKS

In June of 2020, former *New York Times reporter*, Alex Berenson, decided to publish his research and findings in a series of small books called *Unreported Truths About COVID-19 and Lockdowns*. He did it as follows:

Book 1: "Introduction and Death Counts and Estimates" (21 pages) (June 2020)

Book 2: "Update and Examination of Lockdowns as a Strategy" (42 pages) (August 2020)

Book 3: "Masks" (40 pages) (November 2020)

When he released his first book, which is more like a booklet with only 21 pages, he made $100K in the first 30 days in sales. His third book made $120,000 on month one of its release! Isn't that amazing?

I'm not sure what book two made upon its release, because I wasn't tracking it, but right now it's making $60K this month!

Alex decided to write a series of short book because of the fluidity of the subject matter to have updated content as he was writing it.

I'm sharing this story with you because I don't want you to confuse the size of the book with the value it brings. Size has nothing to do with it.

Decide on your topic, do your research to make sure there is a market for it, then write a series of short books for that subject matter.

The more books you write, the more money you will make.

Another huge benefit when you're writing multiple books in the same genre is that you can use information from one book in another book on the same topic. For example, my chapter on Rapid Writing Secrets is included in my books: *28 Books to $100K* and also *Backwards Book Launch*. I didn't have to re-write that section; I just copied and pasted, then tweaked it a bit for the new book.

As you begin writing a series of books, I think at least 25%+ can be repurposed content from your other books.

Here are some examples of authors who have written a successful series of books:

- Author Amy Morin wrote three similar books: *13 Things Mentally Strong People Don't Do*; *13 Things Mental Strong Women Don't Do*; and *13 Things Mentally Strong Parents Don't Do*

- Timothy Ferris wrote: *The 4-Hour Work Week*, *The 4-Hour Chef* and *The 4-Hour Body*

- Robert Kiyosaki wrote a series of *Rich Dad* books such as: *Rich Dad, Poor Dad*; *Rich Dad's Guide to Investing*; *Rich Dad's Cashflow Quadrant*; *Rich Dad's Increase Your Financial IQ*; *Rich Dad's Before You Quit Your Job*; *Rich Dad's Retire Young*; *Retire Rich*; *Rich Dad's Guide to Becoming Rich Without Cutting Up Your Credit Cards* and more!

- Steve Scott writes about Habits in his books: *Habit Stacking*; *Mindful Relationship Habits*; *Bad Habits No More*; and *Stack Your Savings to Build the Money Saving Habit.*

- Seth Godin writes dozens of books about sales and marketing: *The Dip*; *The Purple Cow*; *Linchpin*; *All Marketers are ~~Liars~~ Tell Stories*; *Permission Marketing*, and more.

- Hal Elrod writes dozens of books about *The Miracle Morning*: *The Miracle Morning for Entrepreneurs*; *The Miracle Morning for Writers*; *The Miracle Morning for Network Marketers*; *The Miracle Morning for Sales People*, and more.

REMEMBER THIS: Volume boosts visibility!

Write more books, attract more readers, make more money!

CHAPTER 8

HOW TO WRITE SHORT BOOKS FAST

"One of my books took more than a year to write, ten hours a day. Another took three weeks. Both sell for the same price. The quicker one outsold the other 20 to 1.

A $200 bottle of wine costs almost exactly as much to make as a $35 bottle of wine.

The cost of something is largely irrelevant, people are paying attention to its value.

Your customers don't care what it took for you to make something. They care about what it does for them."

~Seth Godin, Multiple Bestselling Author

In the past, big publishing houses could charge more for longer books. There was also a high demand from consumers who wanted to read longer books. However, times have changed, and people now have less time and decreased attention spans.

Readers want short books!

Top 10 Reasons to Write Short Books

1. Time and attention are in short supply, so there is a greater demand from readers for quick reads.

2. Writing short books focused on one topic is easier than writing a long book with multiple topics.

3. Fewer words require less time to write (it took me seven days to write the bulk of this book.)

4. Volume boosts your visibility (especially on Amazon). You can attract repeat readers who will follow you and consume all of your books.

5. Short books involve less risk. Because you are not investing a considerable amount of time or money in creating these books, less than expected sales will not greatly impact you. You will learn what works and what doesn't work and use that knowledge when writing additional books.

6. You can create a series of short books that explore your favorite subjects in greater depth than you could do in one chapter of a single, longer book.

7. In this article[1], much of the data shows that people do not finish reading books. Since shorter books require less time to read, there is a greater chance people will actually read your entire book.

---

[1] https://www.theifod.com/how-many-people-finish-books/

8. Amazon has a specific category for these books called "Short Reads." You can't select this category when publishing on KDP, but if the number of pages in your book matches the criteria in that Short Reads category, Amazon will automatically include your book in that category giving it more exposure.

9. You can set a lower price for your eBook and get a higher quantity of sales.

10. You can *niche and grow rich* by writing short books in very narrow categories and do exceptionally well.

I love writing shorter books!

I spent over a year writing the second edition of my book, *Quit Your Job and Follow Your Dreams*, which ended up being 250 pages!

When I decided to do the "book a month" experiment, I wrote *How to Find Your Passion: 23 Questions that Can Change Your Entire Life* in about three weeks. I published it within 30 days, and right now, it is one of my bestselling books. It outsells *Quit Your Job and Follow Your Dreams* 10 to 1. I believe it's because people want shorter books with action items that they can use to get quick results.

Of course, some books will do better than others. You never know which topic will appeal best to your readers. The market decides. All you can do is write the best book possible, do your research, launch like a pro, and then move on to the next one.

We live in a high-tech, fast-paced world. Most of us are extremely distracted and our time is fragmented. Gone are the days when people will buy a manifesto and block out their entire weekend to leisurely read long books.

These days, our time is broken up into short and often disjointed periods. We face constant interruptions from emails, texts, phone calls, Facebook, Twitter, Instagram, and more.

Consequently, attention spans have diminished. The desire to learn new things still exists, but most people want to learn faster.

Consider this when writing books. Instead of writing a book on the A-Z of Marketing, write a series of short books focusing on one narrow topic. For example, the marketing series could include books on these topics: Writing Persuasive Sales copy; Creating Facebook Ads; Building a Profitable Blog; How to Create a Webinar, etc.

Think micro-topics instead of macro-topics.

6 Types of Easy-to-Write Short Books

1. List or tip book

2. Step-by-step guide

3. Q&A interview focused on a specific topic

4. Single-question deep dive

5. Collection book (for example, top strategies, top recipes, or top performers in an industry)

6. Extended blog post – if you have a popular blog post, expand on it and publish it as a short book

Return on Investment (ROI)

I've written long books and short books, and shorter books provide a much better return on investment.

Writing shorter books saves you time while increasing your revenue. For example, let's say you spend one full year writing a book (like many of my clients have done), and you earn $200 a month from that one book. If you were writing a book a month, you could have written 12 books, each making $200 a month, and your income would be $2,400 per month instead of $200 per month!

Moreover, you are more likely to finish writing and publishing a shorter book because writing 50,000 to 100,000 words can be a daunting task. My books are usually 15,000 to 20,000 words.

I work with clients who have spent years working on their "one book." I encourage you to write short books. You can write the book in about two weeks, and the editing process will be much quicker.

When I send my final manuscript to my editor (I recommend always using a professional editor), she reads it and sends it back to me with changes marked in the document. I review her suggested changes and accept or reject them. Then, I wait a day or two and read the book cover-to-cover (which is easy to do with a short book), and I always find more typos and changes I want to make.

A 250+ page book would require too much time to write, edit, and review, and I would not be able to publish a book a month if I were writing long books.

So, keep it short and save yourself the overwhelm! Readers want short books!

A while back I developed 16 Rapid Writing Secrets to help my clients go from the blank page to a completed manuscript and I want to share them with you here:

16 RAPID WRITING SECRETS

1. SPEAK YOUR BOOK

Many of my clients do NOT like to sit down and write. So, I have them record what they want to include in their book and then have the recordings transcribed. An editor or assistant puts all the recordings in a cohesive order and creates the book. You can do this yourself by downloading the "Rev" app to your smartphone. Then, create recordings for your book and have them transcribed. This is a very quick way to get your book done!

2. HAVE SOMEONE INTERVIEW YOU

Have someone who isn't familiar with your topic interview you about it. Come up with questions for them to ask you and record the answers and then have them transcribed.

3. WRITE THE FIRST PARAGRAPH

When writing a book, the hardest part is writing the first paragraph. Once it's written, though, the rest will flow. You can even write the first paragraph for each chapter and then go back and add the remaining content. Also, you don't have to write the chapters in the order they will appear in the book. Start with the chapters that you feel the most energy around.

4. WRITE THE CHAPTER SUMMARY FIRST

Many books write themselves once you start writing, so creating a chapter summary will help get the ideas out of your head and give you a place to start.

5. WRITE IN A FRESH ENVIRONMENT

Because of distractions at home, you might get more writing done away from your home office. Go to a coffee shop, your local bookstore, or sit outside, anywhere that you won't be distracted from writing.

6. WRITE IT OUT OF SEQUENCE

Many writers get too focused on the sequence of the chapters and never write anything. That's why you need an editor who will review your book and move things around if they seem out of sequence. Or you can move the chapters around yourself once you've written them all. Don't be too concerned about the order of the chapters because the main goal is to get it out of your head. For me, trying to figure out the sequence as I'm writing slows me down tremendously. Just knowing I can rearrange the chapters when I'm done allows my writing to flow with ease!

7. WRITE WHERE THE EMOTION IS

You should write about a topic that you have strong emotion around because it is important to connect with your readers' emotions. Write down ideas that are high on your emotional scale. You've probably heard, "Make Your Mess Your Message." What messes can you write about?

8. WRITE THE STORIES FIRST, THEN MAKE YOUR POINTS

Everyone loves a good story. People easily remember stories more than a list of facts. There is power in the phrase, "Once upon a time..." So, write your stories first, and then add the points.

Method:

1. Write a Story.

2. Make three points.

3. Rinse and Repeat.

That's it!

9. KEEP AN IDEA OR BRAINSTORMING JOURNAL

Once you decide on the book topic, you'll start getting ideas when you're out walking, showering, drinking a cup of coffee or tea, eating a meal, etc. As these ideas come to you, write them in a journal (let your subconscious write your book for you). When we aren't trying to *chase* ideas, they will often come to us effortlessly.

10. TEXT YOUR BOOK TO YOURSELF OR USE THE NOTES APP

When we text others, we get right to the point. Text your book via the "Notes" app on your smart phone instead of sitting in front of a computer staring at a blank page. Sometimes, we need to trick our brain in order to get things done.

11. WRITE YOUR BOOK WITH POST-IT NOTES

I've used this method and it's amazing. You'll need some Post-it Notes and something to stick them on to like a poster board or a white board. Do a brain dump and write everything you can think of about your topic on each Post-it Note. Then, sort them out and group them together around a theme to create the outline for your book.

12. BLOG YOUR BOOK

I have done a couple of books for clients who collected past blog posts they have written, edited, rearranged, added new content, and included it in a book.

13. PODCAST YOUR BOOK

If you have a podcast, transcribe each episode and use it for a book chapter, and voilà, you have a book!

14. POWERPOINT YOUR BOOK

Many people love using PowerPoint to create content, so why not use it to write your book? Create a slide for each topic in your book, then fill it in with more details.

15. START WITH POWERFUL QUOTES

When I see a great quote, I feel inspired. Many books I've read include a powerful quote at the beginning of each chapter. An easy way to get your book started is to collect 10-12 quotes related to your topic and write a chapter based on each of those quotes.

16. WRITE YOUR BOOK WITH BLOCK TIME

We do our best work when we are in a "FLOW" state, which is when we are completely absorbed in the activity at hand (also known as being "in the zone"). To accomplish this:

- Do your highest value work early in the day.
- Set this time aside as your *block time*.
- Don't do any tasks that are distracting beforehand (email, watching the news, scrolling through social media, etc.).

What are your favorite *Rapid Writing Secrets*?

My Top 4 are:

1. Start with a powerful quote

2. Write the first paragraph

3. Write it out of sequence

4. Write your book on Post-it Notes

Use what works best for you and have fun!

CHAPTER 9

HOW TO GET A BOOK ON WALL STREET JOURNAL AND USA TODAY BESTSELLER LISTS

In 2018, a client hired me to help him publish and launch his book to the #1 bestsellers list on Amazon. His book did phenomenally well! He went on to earn more than $20,000 in royalties from the sales of his book.

Two months after the Amazon launch, he said, "Michelle, I want to become a Wall Street Journal and USA Today bestselling author. Can you help me?"

I kindly explained to him that I didn't know how to do that.

Being a astute and successful multi-millionaire businessman, he said, "Figure it out, and I'll pay you."

That led me to doing a lot of research, trying to crack the code on what it takes to hit these prominent lists. It's a good thing I have 17 years of legal experience as a paralegal and I love doing research!

Luckily, I connected with another author, wo become my business partner, who had four business books published by Wiley and had figured out the exact numbers needed to hit these lists as he had done it for his own books.

My client hired "us," and we relaunched his book to get it on the Wall Street Journal and USA Today bestsellers lists.

I'm happy to tell you that we hit both lists!

I was surprised because I wasn't totally convinced that we could do this since his book was already published and we couldn't release it as a "pre-order."

Most big publishing houses do "pre-orders" for books because it's easier to release the book once you hit the magic numbers you need to make these lists.

Amazon allows you to do a pre-order for up to 12 months prior to the book's release. That gives you a lot of time to get the magic number to hit these lists.

Still, there are many variables that you have no control over when trying to hit these lists, such as:

- Other books being launched the same week as yours (some by big publishing houses).
- Books that are counted (or not counted) and recorded through Nielson Bookscan.
- The number of people that will click the BUY NOW button.
- The publishers of these lists don't have to include your book on the bestsellers list, even if you hit the numbers; they are somewhat curated.

- Unrecorded sales during launch week because of computer errors, glitches, or unknown reasons.

The magic number we were trying to hit for this launch was 6000 sales in one week.

When doing this type of launch, you need to sell 500 or more copies of your book on another platform besides Amazon, such as:

- Barnes and Noble
- Apple iBooks

It may not sound like a lot of sales, but it's not easy to get 500 sales on these platforms because people are conditioned to go to Amazon for books, and Amazon gets the majority of book sales.

Also, for this particular client, we were trying to hit the combined *print and eBook* "Bestsellers list" for the Wall Street Journal.

To hit this combined list, sales of the print book must be recorded via Neilson Bookscan in multiple locations across the country.

Somehow, we pulled it off with an already published book.

Since then, we've done half a dozen more launches and hit the Wall Street Journal bestseller list for every client. For some clients, we hit the USA Today bestseller list as well.

I recommend you only focus on the eBook and do a pre-order launch if you want to hit these lists. Of course, you want the print book available and for sale during the launch, because you absolutely will get sales for it. The goal is to get 6000 eBook sales during the 7-day launch with the eBook available at a discounted price of $.99.

So, I'm sure you're wondering how to get 6000 eBook sales in one week?

It's not easy, but it is essentially a numbers game.

My business partner has a 5 million-plus subscriber list, and we know based on data, we can hit the magic number if we have a great book that appeals to readers. We also do massive marketing during that week.

There are also unknown factors that can affect your launch.

For example, does it matter if you are a self-published author?

I don't believe it matters because self-publishing has become more mainstream. However, I think it's a good idea to create an imprint when publishing and launching to hit these prominent lists.

Using an imprint looks more professional on the book detail page rather than showing up as "Amazon" as your publisher or your name.

If you don't have a 5 million-plus subscriber database and aren't an experienced online marketer, it's probably not going to happen organically without help from someone who has a big list and has done it.

There are a lot of moving parts, and you need a team to make this happen (in my opinion).

My business partner and I take a handful of select books each year to hit the Wall Street Journal and USA Today bestseller lists.

If you are interested in hitting these lists, you can apply here to speak with me:

https://bestsellingauthorprogram.com/wsj-application/

If you have a marketing partner with a huge subscriber list, you can potentially do this on your own with a pre-order by taking the following steps:

1. Make your book available for pre-order at least 60 days before launch week.

   Note: I don't recommend launching in December because you will be competing with the biggest publishing houses and holiday book releases.

2. Price your eBook at $.99. If the publisher doesn't want to set the initial price this low, you can price it higher until a few days before launch week.

3. Make sure your book is available on as many platforms as possible, such as Barnes & Noble, Books-A-Million, Apple, Walmart, etc. You can do this through expanded distribu-

tion on KDP or using Ingram Sparks, who is one of the largest book distributors. I have several clients who published their eBook on KDP and their print book on Ingram Sparks for broader distribution.

4. Although you can't get "reviews" on a pre-order eBook, you can release your print book on Amazon or Ingram Sparks and get reviews, which will appear on your Amazon product page. Having good reviews (at least a dozen) will help your book during the launch.

5. Use your own imprint. Research imprint names to ensure the name you selected is not in use by someone else.

6. Make sure your social media platforms are all up to date and look good since Wall Street Journal and/or USA Today may be looking closely at you.

7. Have a professional website with a place for readers to subscribe to your email list

8. Choose the right keywords and categories for your launch so that your book will show up on as many bestsellers lists on Amazon as possible.

9. Promote your book to get all the sales during launch week and hit the magic number of 6000. You can use paid promoters during this week and run paid ads on Amazon, Facebook, and Book Bub.

Remember, if this were easy, everyone would be doing it. It's not easy, and it requires a lot of coordination and strategy. We only take on books that we think can hit these lists.

If you really want to elevate your title and be seen as the go-to expert in your field, and you have a high-ticket offer to make money on the back end, then I think becoming a Wall Street Journal and/or USA Today bestselling author is worth it.

Most business authors focus on Wall Street Journal bestsellers list, but it's also a big achievement to hit the USA Today bestsellers list.

The USA Today bestsellers list is different in that it includes the top 150 books in all genres across the entire country for that week. Essentially, your business book could be on a list with children's books, fiction books, etc. In other words, you're competing with a lot of different genres.

This is how you become a Wall Street Journal and USA Today bestselling author.

CHAPTER 10

CLOSING THOUGHTS

Becoming a bestselling author doesn't automatically mean you will get rich. The reality is your bestselling book could make $200 a month or it could make $100,000 a month. The market decides what it wants, but you have to help the "market" and readers find your book and you do that by following all the steps I've outlined in this book.

If you are serious about reaching more people and making money as an author, then you should consider writing more books. The more books you write, the more money you will make from each of those books.

Additionally, when you write books in series and have multiple books on the same bestsellers lists, you will get repeat readers who will read all the books in your series.

Nothing is guaranteed. I like to look at everything in my business as an *experiment*. I see what works, and what doesn't work, adjust, and go from there.

I love writing and creating, so I'm having fun. I'm teaching what I know, what I've done, what's worked and what hasn't worked, and my goal is to help other authors do the same.

If you write one book and think you're going to get rich from that, I think you will be greatly disappointed. I do have clients who have one book, in multiple formats, making $2000-$4000 per month. But it took time to hit those numbers – time spent running Amazon ads, doing podcast interviews, marketing books, selling programs and courses, and blogging, etc.

To be successful you have to be in this for the long haul and, as with every new endeavor, there is a learning curve. It takes discipline, commitment, and a lot of work to be successful as an author. I'll admit, there were times when my sales were low that I wanted to give up, but I didn't.

The more books I write, the better my writing gets, and the more people I will reach.

I'm writing this book in November 2020, and this the 11th book I've written this year. I have one more to write for December, and when I'm done, I'll have written a book a month for a year! Now, I can take those 12 books I've written to create audiobooks, workbooks, journals, box sets, and more to generate more income and attract more readers. Next year, I will focus on my top-selling books to create more re-purposed content.

I hope I've inspired you to dream big, become a creator, and share your message with the world.

Here's to your success!

Michelle Kulp

BONUS

MICHELLE'S PRIVATE AND VETTED ROLODEX

It can take years to find great book promoters, formatters, editors, and cover designers. I currently use the following resources for my books, or these have been recommended to me by other authors.

PROMOTERS: PAID VS. FREE

It's important to understand that there are promoters who will only promote your book when it is free (which you can do by signing up for Amazon's Kindle Select program inside your KDP account) and there are other promoters who only do paid (which typically means your book price is reduced to $.99). Last, there are some promoters that do free and paid launches. I just wanted to point this out.

Promoters for FREE Book Launches

- RobinReads.com/genre-divide/
- BookTweeters.com/ - home –
- eReaderIQ.com/authors/submissions/dds/
- Fiverr.com/bknights
- JamesHMayfield.com/book-promotions/ *only does free
- FreeBooksy.com/freebooksy-feature-pricing/m

Promoters for Books Priced at Least $.99

***Instead of freebooksy, hire bargainbooksy:

- BargainBooksy.com/sell-more-books-2/
- BookSends.com/advertise.php
- eReaderNewsToday.com/bargain-and-free-book-submissions/ - toggle-id-1 – *****must be submitted 10-14 days in advance!

*90 days after you do a #1 book launch, you can apply for a BookBub featured deal:

- BookBub Featured Deal, Price Varies: BookBub.com/partners/pricing

**If you don't get accepted, try running ads on their platform:

- BookBub Ads Anytime, Price Varies: Insights.BookBub.com/introducing-bookbub-ads-promote-any-book-any-time/

BOOK COVER DESIGNERS

- 99designs.com/ebook-cover-design
- 100covers.com
- FosterCovers.com
- GraceMyCanvas.com
- Archangelink.com/book-covers/
- FionaJaydeMedia.com/non-fiction/

- Fiverr.com/designa2z
- Fiverr.com/cal5086
- Fiverr.com/galuhh
- Fiverr.com/lauria
- Fiverr.com/vikiana
- Fiverr.com/germancreative
- My designer is Zeljka: vukojeviczeljka@gmail.com

FORMATTERS

- **Heather Mize at My Book Team** – heather@MyBookTeam.com

TEMPLATES:

For DIY formatting, you can get some great templates at BookDesignTemplates.com

EDITORS (All editors I have used)

- **Heather Mize** – heather@MyBookTeam.com
- **Lori Duff, Esq** – lori@loriduffwrites.com
- **Pamela Gossiaux** – pam@pamelagossiaux.com
- **Hollace Donner** – Pailmoritz@yahoo.com

PROOFREADER

- Kimberly Marzullo, kimberlymarzullo@icloud.com

GHOSTWRITERS

- **Lori Duff, Esq.** – LoriDuffWrites.com/lori-writes-for-you-expert-ghost-writer/ghost-writing-rates
- **Emily Crookston, Ph.D.** – ThePocketPHD.com

COPYWRITERS

- Rob Schultz – ProfitSeduction.com
- BestPageForward.net/blurbs

AMAZON ADS

- **Alex Strathdee** – AdvancedAmazonAds.com

ONLINE COURSE PLATFORM

- **I use Thinkific** for my "Client Learning Portal," which is essentially my online course/program/training: http://try.thinkific.com/michellekulp6975

PUBLIC RELATIONS

- **Christina Daves** – www.ChristinaDaves.com

SOFTWARE I USE

- ***Aweber:** http://michellekulp.aweber.com
- ***Bluehost:** http://www.bluehost.com/track/mkulp
- ***Pop-Up domination:** https://app.popupdomination.com/aff/5d4a184df5895d7c596f5242

- ***Publisher Rocket**
  https://mkulp--rocket.thrivecart.com/publisher-rocket/

- **KDSpy**
  https://mkulp--leadsclick.thrivecart.com/kdspy-v5/

- **Bestseller Ranking Pro:**
  https://mkulp--tckpublishing.thrivecart.com/bestseller-ranking-pro-special-lifetime/

- **Book Report**: https://app.getbookreport.com/

- **HTML Book Description Generator**:
  https://kindlepreneur.com/amazon-book-description-generator/

BOOK PRINTERS:

- http://www.printopya.com/book

ILLUSTRATORS

- www.Gemini-h.com/illustrations
- www.Instagram.com/art_of_geminih

www.ingramcontent.com/pod-product-compliance
Lightning Source LLC
Chambersburg PA
CBHW060617200326
41521CB00007B/795